THE ADVENTURES OF ROBIN HOOD

E. CHARLES VIVIAN

Introduction

So little is left of the England that Robin Hood and his merry men knew that it is doubtful if anyone of today would recognize it if it were possible to go to sleep in our England and to wake up in his.

The greater part of the old ballads, in which the stories of the famous outlaw are to be found, fix his outlawry as happening in the reign of King Richard Lion Heart, who, when he went off to the crusade in the Holy Land, left England in charge of his bad brother John. And, both in his regency for Richard and when he came to reign as king, John proved himself the worst monarch England has ever had.

The people whom Richard and John ruled were by no means a united nation, as the English are today. In the Midlands, where Robin gathered his band, there were many Saxon families who hated the Normans as conquerors and oppressors.

The Normans when they first came ruled by fear over their Saxon subjects. In order to bind his followers closely to him, William the Conqueror had given them great estates all over the country, thrusting out the Saxon lords who were the real owners, and enslaving their men. With their own followers, and with the wealth they won from their holdings, the Norman lords became so powerful that even their kings feared them.

In the reign of King Stephen came years of war which ruined whole counties, and left starving and desperate men throughout England. The Norman barons set up great castles all over the country, and from these, with their men-at-arms, they terrorized the Saxon cultivators of the land, robbed them of their crops and farming stock, and defied even the King.

Henry II made things a little better, but not much, for he was concerned over his French possessions as much as over his English lands. He curbed the power of the barons to some extent, and the common people who tilled the land began to breathe rather more easily and to reckon that their worst times were past. When King Henry died the English hoped much from King Richard, a strong, just man. But he went over to his lands in France very soon after his coronation, and left the people at the mercy of John, his brother.

John was not only bad but weak as well. He yielded to favourite nobles, gave away lands to win followers, being afraid of the time when Richard should return and call him to account.

All over the country great castles went up again, most of them no better than nests of robbers. If one of the barons saw a farm that he coveted, he brought some accusation against its owner, had him flung into prison, and took the farm. For before the signing of Magna Charta a man could be seized and thrown into prison, and left there till the end of his life without trial.

Most of the barons had power of life and death on their own estates. They could not only imprison any of their followers but could inflict any punishment up to hanging.

In later days the Church provided some refuge for oppressed people, but in this age the offices of the Church were mainly in the hands of Norman prelates, who had little or no sympathy with the descendants of the conquered Saxons. Abbeys and monasteries held great tracts of land, to which some baron was appointed steward, as was the Guy of Gisborne, who was one of Robin Hood's greatest enemies.

Most harsh and unjust of all, in the eyes of the Saxons, were the game laws by which the Norman kings tried to reserve all the game to themselves. All deer were the property of the King, and if any of his subjects shot an arrow at a buck without leave, he was liable to have his right hand cut off. For a second offence he might have his eyes put out, and for certain offences the punishment was death.

Starving men, with hungry children at home, saw fat deer ranging the forests, and often the temptation was too great for them. They had been robbed of everything by the followers of the Kings who made these laws, and for the sake of a good meal they took the deer, risking even life itself to feed their starving little ones.

Swift and sure punishment often followed. Women and children were turned out from their hovels to starve by the roadside, while the father swung a corpse on some baron's gallows. Nobody dared give help to these suffering ones.

Now the England in which these things happened was a country that we, who travel about as we like, and have freedom in every way, can hardly understand. No serf who worked on the land might leave his lord's estate to work for anyone else, for he was his lord's property. There were great forests over much of the country; there were no roads, only rutted tracks leading from one big town to another. A journey of twenty miles was a great adventure, only to be undertaken after much thought, and with fear of the outlaws and robbers who infested every path. For safety, men travelled in companies, when they travelled at all, and it was very rare for a common man to have been as much as five miles from his own village.

Between these villages lay great tracts of waste land, and here and there throughout the country were vast forests, like the Forest of Sherwood into which Robin Hood retreated when he was outlawed. There were few paths through these forests; they were made up of thickets and gloomy woods, and green glades in which the deer fed, far from the sight of men. Wardens, as they were called, were appointed by the King to see that the game laws were not broken, and these wardens appointed foresters or rangers to patrol the neighbourhood of the villages.

This was the England of Robin Hood, a country in which a man could hardly call his soul his own unless he were a baron.

Sherwood Forest stretched up from the neighbourhood

of Nottingham towards the little collection of huts that stood where Sheffield stands today. No man knew all its depths, and parts of it were believed to be enchanted, haunted by gnomes and elves and even fiery dragons. Here and there lived bands of desperate men, driven out from their villages in fear of their lives, ready to pounce on any travellers and rob them of all they possessed. These men were safe in the forest.

Saxon and Norman alike looked for the return of King Richard, and hoped for better times with his coming. While they hoped, the barons and even the great churchmen ground the poor into lower depths, so that life became harder still.

Then came Robin Hood, born a freeman—that is to say, he had never been a serf, but held his own land. He was an adventurous sort of man even in his youth, and knew as much as anyone of the intricacies of Sherwood Forest. A friend of the poor, and one who hated injustice, he made many friends, farmed his land, and treated his men fairly. Often he talked of equal justice for rich and poor, but in the beginning it was only talk, for such a thing seemed impossible. Most of all, he hated the unjust game laws. So things stood, with little law and still less justice in England, when Robin Hood was young.

THE
ADVENTURES OF
ROBIN HOOD

E. CHARLES VIVIAN

With Illustrations by
JULES GOTLIEB

AIRMONT BOOKS
401 LAFAYETTE ST. • **NEW YORK, N. Y. 10003**

An Airmont Classic
specially selected for the Airmont Library
from the immortal literature of the world

PRINTED IN THE UNITED STATES OF AMERICA

AIRMONT PUBLISHING CO., INC., New York, N.Y.

CONTENTS

Chapter

CHAPTER I / How Sebald the Serf Got Food

WHITE winter lay heavily on Sherwood Forest, and far across the moors to the North Country where Whitby Abbey towered over the sea. Winter had been cruelly long that year, and now, though the time of spring sowing was near, there was no sign of the bitter cold relaxing.

A bare stone's throw into the Forest, on the edge of the lands that Guy of Gisborne stewarded for the rich Abbey of St. Mary's, a ragged figure skulked among the trees. Shreds of what had once been clothes hung about him as Sebald the Dolt glanced down the forest aisles, or crouched among the snow-laden undergrowth; about his legs and feet were tied wisps of dead grass for warmth, and as he moved he left little specks of red in each footprint, for the dead stalks and twigs had pierced the soles of his numbed feet. On and on he moved, away from the open lands and into the depths of the Forest.

Then he stiffened to absolute stillness, for, moving down wind, a dozen head of deer came, nosing at the snow for food, unconscious of his presence. They saw him too late for one of their number, for Sebald stepped out from behind the tree that had hidden him, lifted his bow and let fly; a young stag went down, kicking, and the rest of the deer vanished before·Sebald could reach the wounded thing and end his work with a knife.

Working like a madman, he ripped the skin from the haunch of the dead beast, cut a slice of the warm flesh, and bolted it as a dog might have done. After that, he went at the carcase more carefully, cutting off the best of the meat and placing it in a pile on the snow, strip after strip of juicy venison. Then, with a cry that was more like a dog's bark, he started up, knife in hand, and faced the tall man whose shadow had fallen across him as he worked.

A young man, this new-comer, with reddish hair, a little pointed beard, and a lithe, muscular figure that betokened more than usual strength and quickness. Sebald faced him with knife upraised and terror in his gaunt face, of which every line told of hunger and fear.

"Put the knife down, Sebald," said the tall man quietly.

"Robin—Robin of Locksley!" Sebald gasped. "Master, I was starved."

"And like to be hanged," said Robin of Locksley. "For this is death, Sebald, if a forester find one head of deer taken."

"If I die of a rope, or of hunger, what difference is there?" Sebald asked doggedly. "Look you, Master Robin, when this winter began I had a wife and two little ones. But because I fell ill, a thing no serf may do, Guy of Gisborne turned us out of our hut and gave our shelter to Walter the Bald. A serf who cannot work, said Guy, shall neither eat nor shelter on his lands, and they drove us out, the wife and the children with me, though the little ones were all unfit."

"True," said Robin, nodding. "Guy of Gisborne is a

hard man, and cruel. But it is death to touch the deer, Sebald."

"Death? What is death but a kindness?" Sebald asked. "For so my wife found it when the cold wrapped her round and she fell asleep, never to wake more in this world. So the child Freda found it, for at least she will hunger no more, and now only the boy Waltheof is left me, and he a-crying with bitter hunger. By the Rood, Master Robin, if I hang, I hang with a full belly, and the boy shall have one more good meal!"

There was a look of pity in Robin's eyes. "Where is the boy?" he asked.

"There"—Sebald pointed along the way he had come—"in the hollow of a dead elm, wrapped in such rags as I could find him that he might not die of the cold."

"Then you harbour in the forest?" Robin asked.

Sebald nodded. "Else I must go back to Guy of Gisborne, being his man," he answered. "And to go back means lashes on the back, and labour from morn to night, with more lashes at the end of it, since I am all unhandy and slow, and so they call me the dolt, Master Robin. I tell you"—his voice rose to sudden fierceness—"there is no justice for us Saxon English under these dogs of Normans!"

"It is true," Robin answered moodily. "But look you, Sebald, bring the lad with you and come to my farm. We may then decide what can best be done for you."

Sebald looked incredulous. "To your farm, Master Robin? But—but I have killed the king's deer!"

A slow smile grew in Robin's eyes. "I may have loosed a shaft or two myself, at times, good Sebald," he said, "for the deer take toll of my crops without payment. Bring the boy and come—there is at the least a shelter among the cattle where he may keep warm."

"Master Robin," said Sebald, with tears in his eyes, "well do they say you've the kindest heart 'twixt Nottingham and York."

"Tush, man!" said Robin, and turned away. "Follow when you will, and come to me. I will have speech of Guy of Gisborne, and see if I may not keep you among my men."

He turned away then, and went out from the forest and across the open to where, a couple of miles away, rose a stout wooden dwelling with its stables and byres and ricks about it. Here Robin of Locksley had lived alone since his father's death, a freeman holding his two hundred acres of land under the Abbey of St. Mary's. His grandfather, in the time of Henry the First, had been granted the tenancy of this acreage, the best of all the lands belonging to the Abbey, and when Robin's father died Guy of Gisborne had tried vainly to thrust Robin out from his holding and take back the farm to the Abbey's use.

Now, as Robin went slowly back, thinking bitterly over the wrongs of men like Sebald, he left one track of footprints straight from the carcase of the deer to his own homestead. Presently came Sebald with his boy Waltheof, a lad of ten who shivered and even cried with the cold as he kept beside his father, and they left two more tracks in the snow.

Late that afternoon came Herbert the ranger along the edge of the forest, where Robin's lands began, and when he came to the tracks in the snow he stopped and looked down. There was the clear, long-striding track of Robin's shod feet, and Herbert passed by that, knowing whose feet had made it. Then he came on the shapeless blurs made by Sebald's grass-wrapped feet, and beside them the small indentations where the child Waltheof had walked. Herbert saw red blots in the snow, where Sebald's torn feet had bled.

"Ha!" he said. "There has been a killing here!"

So he turned into the forest, following on the tracks, and came to the hollow elm where Sebald had left his boy. Thence he followed on, and came to a place where the snow was all disturbed and thrown about, and at one place had been made into a mound on which were still the traces of Sebald's hands.

"A killing," said Herbert to himself, "and a burying too."

He grubbed in the mound with his hands, and presently came on a two-tined antler. Grasping it, he dragged forth all that Sebald had left of the deer's carcase, and stared down at it as it lay before him.

"So!" said Herbert. "Master and man together go a-hunting! Fine news for Sir Guy! I think he will have Robin's farm at last, and for this news he will make me bailiff."

He slung the carcase across his shoulders and hurried off to Fosse Grange, as Guy of Gisborne's strong house of stone was named, since it stood by the old fosse that runs from the Abbey of St. Mary's down toward Newark. It was all but a castle, this hold from which Guy ruled the lands of St. Mary's for Hugo de Rainault, the Norman abbot who had been granted rule of St. Mary's while Henry Curtmantle was yet alive.

A tall man and a fierce was Guy, swarthy and sneering, a hater of Saxons, at whom he was wont to jeer as he told how his grandfather had seen their sires run from Senlac when their Harold died.

Into Guy's hall strode Herbert the ranger, the deer still across his shoulders. At the back of the hall was a great roaring fire of logs, before which stood Guy of Gisborne himself, warming his hands behind his back. To him went Herbert, and laid the deer before him.

"How now, man—how now?" growled Guy. "Who has been gnawing at that meat? Why is it not a whole carcase?"

"Because Robin of Locksley has gnawed it," said Herbert.

"Ha!" said Guy, his eyes alight. "Now by the teeth of St. Peter we have him! Have you proof, Herbert?"

"Proof enough, lord," said Herbert, "for there go his footprints from where the carcase lay buried in the snow, and on across his land to his own door. There went with them the prints made by some lumbering serf and a little lad, whom he got to do the foul work with him. Proof enough, lord."

"Aye," said Guy, "proof enough. We will have Locksley back for the Abbey, and we will have, too, the hand of Master Robin chopped from him, or I think, with a word from Abbot Hugo, I may get leave to tear out his eyes. The Saxon hound has flouted us long enough, eh, Herbert?"

"Full long, Lord Guy," Herbert agreed. "And I shall be bailiff of Locksley, an it please you?"

"That is for Abbot Hugo to settle," Guy answered, "but a word from me to him shall be your reward for this news. Now away with you while I arm," Guy ordered. "Bid a dozen of our men-at-arms get mailed, and saddle me my roan horse, and I warrant you Locksley farm shall lack a tenant before the sun reddens to-morrow's snow. Hasten good Herbert, if you would see your vacant bailiffship waiting."

He put on a suit of mail while Herbert gathered the men, and an hour before sunset they rode out from the Fosse Grange toward Locksley farm. The afternoon had gone grey and sullen, with a moist wind under which the snow began to soften to slush, and the heavily armed retainers laboured panting behind Guy's strong horse on their way to their task.

In an empty byre at Locksley farm the boy Waltheof slept amid warm straw, full-fed for the first time that winter, while Sebald dozed beside him, fed and content too. In the stout porch of the homestead stood Robin, looking up at the sky and snuffing the wind.

"A week of this," he said to himself, "and we shall be sowing our barley. It is winter's end, for a certainty."

Then he saw how, across the whiteness of the open between the farmstead and the forest edge, came a little company of men plodding through the snow. They took no note of the winding track by which they should have come, but marched straight across the ploughed fields.

"Now what do these Norman hogs want?" Robin muttered angrily. "Must they tear up my young wheat with their clumsy hooves to come at me?"

CHAPTER 2 / How Robin Took
to the Woods

GUY OF GISBORNE and his men were still a mile away when Robin's keen eyes—such eyes as were seldom equalled for their sure vision—picked out Guy as the leader of the band, and on the instant Robin linked up his glimpse of Herbert the ranger gazing at the house a while earlier, Sebald sheltering in the byre, and the carcase of the deer that Sebald had brought down.

He stepped back into the house, buckled on his sword, and reached for his long bow and its quiver. He had Will Scarlett, his head man, armed in like fashion and out rousing the serfs while Guy and his band were still half a mile distant.

He had with him Will Scarlett on his right, and on his left was a fat youth with a great yew bow. This lad was Much, son of old Much the miller, who should have been helping his father at the mill, but had stolen away to drink ale with Scarlett instead, being a lazy lad by nature. Yet, having drunk Robin's ale, he took his bow and stood by Robin now trouble threatened, though he knew nothing of the nature of the trouble.

Behind these three were six of Robin's serfs who could handle either bow or quarter staff well, since Robin always encouraged such play among them, not knowing when it might be useful. So stood the nine of them, with Sebald crouching somewhere in the rear, when Guy of Gisborne rode into hearing.

Robin laid an arrow on the string and held the bow lightly, as did both Scarlett and Much. Guy, who knew even then what skill the man before him had with the bow, reined in as he saw the arrows fitted.

"Robin of Locksley!" Guy cried out from the barred visor of his helm, "put down your arms and yield you all to me, steward and liege man of Abbot Hugo de Rainault, that you may suffer your due punishment!"

But Robin lifted the bow as if to take aim, and Guy's men-at-arms loosened their shields as they saw it.

"Strong words, steward," Robin answered composedly. "Why and for what should we yield us?"

"For that you and your men have slain the king's deer in this forest of Sherwood," Guy called back. "And for that I declare you, Robin of Locksley, dispossessed of your holding, and to lose your right hand that you may draw bow no more."

"Without trial, steward?" Robin asked incredulously. "Without defence or question you pass judgment and sentence?"

"Trial, hind?" Guy echoed contemptuously. "What think you yourself, a baron of the realm, that you look for trial? The case is proved against you, and in the name of Abbot Hugo I do justice on you and such men as are guilty with you!"

"Justice, you Norman thief?" Robin fired back. "I tell you, Guy of Gisborne, since King Richard went crusading there has been no justice in our England. Let your men come but another ten paces forward and some of you shall never see another day's light!"

Guy sat still on his horse for nearly a minute, then

he beckoned a man of his, who came with shield raised to guard head and breast from any arrow that might fly.

"Loose me a crossbow bolt or two at that tall felon, and make us a free way into Locksley farmstead," Guy bade quietly.

The man stepped back among his fellows, and fitted a bolt to the crossbow behind another's shield. The feathered quarrel hissed viciously, unsuspectedly, and a serf who stood between and a little behind Robin himself and Scarlett crumpled down without a sound, for the point had entered his brain. Without losing sight of Guy's movements, Robin saw the deed.

"First blood!" he cried. "Now guard you, Guy of Gisborne, for here you shall only enter dead."

On the word, he loosed the arrow from his string, and it quivered and stuck in the visor bars of Guy of Gisborne's helm, so strongly shot that Guy reeled and nearly fell from his saddle with the shock. And scarce had that arrow struck before a second shaft from Robin's bow went in at the neck of the crossbowman who had shot the serf, so that the man fell with his life blood pouring out on to the snow.

"Now are we all dead men if they take us," Robin said to his followers, "so shoot hard and often till they come at us, and may the shafts pierce the mail! But do you run, Much, for this is no quarrel of yours."

"I will run," said Much, "no more than a barrel of ale untapped. For here is foul work, and I will not see it done."

At that he loosed his string and sent a shaft humming, to glance off a retainer's shield harmlessly.

Seven other arrows sang through the air, and one of them found the brain of a man-at-arms, and one went through a man's calf, so that he sat down in the snow and squealed as he pulled the shaft out.

"An end of three," said Robin, who grew cool now the fight had begun, "and still stands Locksley untouched." He sighted one man whose crossbow was aimed, and drove off a humming shaft that took the man in the wrist and pierced through flesh and gristle up to his elbow. "Four!" he shouted as the man turned and ran, shrieking. "How like you our welcome, steward? If you get not my right hand, you get the use of it!"

With all his force he loosed another shaft at Guy's helmet, in which the broken end of the first arrow still stuck. This second arrow struck higher, squarely in the front of the steel, which, as Robin knew, it could not pierce, but the force of it was so great that Guy of Gisborne tumbled down into the snow and lay half stunned with the shock. And while he lay, a heap of rags shot out from behind Robin, fled across the intervening space, and a wild scream went up as Sebald the Dolt leaped on Herbert the ranger, a flying fury.

"This for my wife starved!" yelled Sebald, "and this for the child you thrust out into the cold!" And twice the knife with which he had cut up the deer flashed, while Herbert, drawing his dagger even as he stabbed, fell dying, and thrust the dagger into Sebald's heart, so that he too fell, dead, on the body of the man who had turned him out from his hut at Guy of Gisborne's bidding.

There was a tall man of Guy's following who, when his master fell, advanced with drawn sword to stand over him, and presently Guy got on his feet and drew his sword as well. The two of them led on, both covered in mail, against the party in the shadow of the house, among whom were now seven unharmed and two dead by crossbow bolts. But Guy's party had nearly thirty yards to come, against the finest archer who ever drew bow in England, and they came heavily because of the deep, soft snow, while the great arrows hummed toward them. So it was that only these two came up, for of the rest of Guy's men three sat in the snow, sore wounded, and the rest lay dead.

But Guy of Gisborne, trusting in his mail of proof, came on, as did his man, and Much the miller's son ran out with his quarter-staff and thwacked the man across his helm, so that he fell down senseless. But Robin stood against Guy of Gisborne with his sword, and Scarlett and the serfs stood round.

It was a fight of which there could be but one end, for Guy of Gisborne, heavily armed, and but lately stunned by Robin's arrow ringing against his helm, was slow, while Robin skipped round him and struck where he would. At the last Robin lifted his sword and brought it down on the helmet so strongly that the blade snapped, and as Guy staggered Robin flung the useless hilt away and wrenched Guy's own sword out of his grasp.

"Now yield—yield to my justice, steward!" Robin bade.

"Never!" Guy grated back.

"Seize him, Scarlett," said Robin. "To it, serfs, and bind him tightly. There is a reckoning due now."

They grasped and held the man, while Robin himself went off and led in the roan war horse on which

Guy had ridden. He came back with it to where they held Guy of Gisborne prisoner and cursing most foully.

"Cease!" Robin thundered at him. "Are honest serfs to have their ears befouled by such a man as this! By the Rood, steward, death is but an inch distant from thee."

"Kill and make an end," said Guy. "I had as well be dead as shamed."

"Not so," said Robin, "for there has been enough of killing this day, and the shaming is not yet finished. Hark, steward! For this killing I am an outlawed man, and these poor loyal souls with me— that much I know. Abbot Hugo will welcome the excuse, but I have it in mind to send him a messenger of this day's work before the price is set on my head. Lift him on the horse, Scarlett, and face his head toward its tail."

This they did, Scarlett and the serfs heaving most mightily until they had the kicking, struggling steward placed. Then they brought ropes at Robin's bidding, and Much the miller's son lashed Guy's feet tightly under the horse, so that he could not move to dismount.

"Now, steward," said Robin, "ride you thus to Abbot Hugo, or first to your own grange, I care not which. But say to Abbot Hugo that from this day he may take Locksley farm, to the use of the fat thieves that wear the cowl in St. Mary's under him. Tell him, too, that he and his shall pay for the farm, for from this day I declare war on him and all his kind, as on you and your kind, who from behind stone walls ravage honest men. Scarlett, give him a rein in each hand and let him go."

Then Robin picked up the steward's sword and struck the horse across his flank with the flat of it, and Guy rode off, facing toward them, into the darkness, shouting threats of the vengeance of Abbot Hugo until he was out of hearing.

"Now," said Robin, "there is much to do. Let us bury these our men, but leave Guy's men till he come again."

This they did, and when it was over Robin gathered his men in the great front room of the farmstead, and spoke to them by the flickering rushlight while they sat over meat and ale.

"With the dawn comes Guy again," he told them, "and for to-day's work there is torture and a hanging for every man of us, if they find us. As for me, I am for the depths of Sherwood, where no man may track or find us. A free life and an open, lads, with wood aplenty for fires to warm us, and to roast our meat as we bring it down. War on those who have drained our lives of all but labour that they may fatten—who comes with me?"

"I," said Scarlett and Much together, and then all the rest answered too. They were but nine, all told, that followed Robin to the forest at first, but they were brave men all.

"I thank you, friends," he said, "and look for a better life there than we have known yet. Now to take all that we can carry for our comfort, and away. This thaw will hide our tracks. But first do you, Much, take the lad Waltheof to your father's mill, and there leave him to be tended."

By midnight Locksley stead stood empty.

CHAPTER 3 / How Robin Dined
with the Sheriff

It was mid-March when Robin, who knew the forest wilds better than any man of his time, led his nine men to a glade in a valley where a cave at the side gave them shelter, a clear stream provided water, and the deer, plentiful enough, served for meat. For the rest, they had brought all the stores there were in Locksley, and for the time were fed and content.

Robin gathered his nine followers, since no more had yet come to join them, and declared his purpose to them.

"Now look you, my merry men, that you do no harm to yeomen, or to them that till with the plough, or to the knight or squire who is kind to the poor. But these bishops and abbots who rob the poor, and the high sheriffs who bind and beat them, cropping their ears and cruelly ill-treating them, these you shall lighten of their ill-gotten gains. Yet, by the Virgin, you shall never do harm to any woman in the land."

This was the law of the band that Robin formed, and, but a day after he had made it, he and his men lay along the road to Nottingham, being out on a hunt, when the Prior of Newark came down the road with half a dozen baggage mules and monks to lead them, and only a couple of armed retainers of the Priory for guard. Since these two took to their horses' heels at sight of nine resolute bowmen and their hooded leader—for Robin had drawn a hood over his

face before he showed himself—there was no
fighting. But there were two kegs of good wine, and
four hundred marks in gold, and a store of brown
cloth, and bags of good white flour, which Robin
counted up while the Prior and his monks stood by.

"Now, Prior," said Robin, "we will bind you all on
your mules, and give you a hand apiece free to guide
them home, where you may tell that Robin i' the
Hood begins his rule in Sherwood Forest, and war
on all oppressors of the poor."

And, while the disgruntled Prior and his monks
made their sorry way on toward Newark, Robin and
his men retreated to their fastness with this welcome
spoil. From that day the great outlaw began to be
known as Robin i' the Hood, or Robin Hood.

Now, lying up in the forest, they had no news of
what went on in the outer world, and Robin himself
determined to get news in some way. The spring was
still young when, on the track between Mansfield village and Nottingham town, he met with the potter of
Mansfield, who rode in his cart with a load of pots
for sale in Nottingham.

"Now I am a ruined man," said the potter, for he
saw Scarlett and Robin's men lurking beside the
way, and knew himself among outlaws. "For if I lose
my horse and cart——"

"You shall lose nothing by me," Robin promised.
"Sell me the pots at the price you would ask in Nottingham, and I will leave you two gold marks as
surety for the horse and cart. But lend me too your
clothes with the potter's clay on them, lest I should
be known in Nottingham as Robin i' the Hood."

Contented by the sight of the two gold marks and
the price of his pots, the potter made the exchange,

and Robin drove off to Nottingham, leaving the potter with his men till he should return. Having reached the town market-place, he set up his wares at less than half their usual price, and soon sold all the cheaper stuff. But he had left a dozen or so of large dishes.

Now across the market stood the great house of Robert de Rainault, Sheriff of Nottingham and brother to Hugo de Rainault, Abbot of St. Mary's. Robin put his wares in a basket, went across the market-square, and knocked at the sheriff's door. Presently came a serving woman.

"Having traded well in your market," said Robin, with a bow, "I bring these poor vessels as a present for Mistress de Rainault, if she will accept them as a gift."

"A gift from you?" the woman asked.

Robin nodded. "From the potter of Mansfield," he answered, and, leaving the basket, went back to his cart and waited.

Presently the woman came across the square and found him by his cart. "Good potter," she said, "my master thinks it a right welcome gift, for we were short of dishes, and he asks that you come and take meat at his board."

"Gladly," said Robin, "especially if there be ale as well as meat, for crying pots for sale is dry work."

He followed the woman into de Rainault's house, well knowing that its owner would hang him yards high if he guessed his identity. There they gave him a seat at the great board, below the salt, with de Rainault's men, and piled his plate high, with a great horn of ale beside it. Meanwhile de Rainault, seated above the salt with his wife and some friends, talked.

"Forty gold marks," said the Sheriff, "and the crier shall cry it in the town to-day."

"Forty?" said one of his friends. "A high price for any man's head."

"But this is a dangerous man," the Sheriff explained. "He killed seven of Guy of Gisborne's armed followers with his own hand, and made Guy a laughing-stock to boot. And with a great band of seventy or more followers he robbed the Prior of Newark of all the good man possessed."

"Good," said Robin to himself, "the fifty have grown."

"A dangerous villain," said the Sheriff's wife, "let us hope he do not come to Nottingham."

"Let him come!" cried de Rainault. "I would capture him myself, and give you half the forty marks for new dresses."

"Would you though?" said Robin to himself, smiling.

"And to-day," the Sheriff went on, "he shall be cried through the streets of Nottingham as wolf's head, outlaw, for any man to take or kill at sight, with forty marks reward for proof of his death or for his body if captured alive. We must rid our good country of such pests."

Robin got up from the board, having eaten enough, and marched up to stand before the Sheriff, to whom he bowed low.

"Thanks for the good food, lord Sheriff," he said, "and I will now get back to my trade."

"Who are you, and what is your trade?" the Sheriff asked.

"And I trust your noble dame will find my poor

pots welcome," Robin concluded, without answering the question.

"Ha!" said de Rainault, "'tis our potter! The dishes were right welcome, potter, and I trust you have fed well at my board. But now, where do you go?"

"Back to Mansfield, to make more pots, for I have sold all my stock," Robin answered.

"Look to your going, then," the Sheriff warned him, "for there is a most pestilent rogue loose in Sherwood who will rob you of every groat if he find you. We have put out a reward of forty gold marks for his head, and Guy of Gisborne is assembling a band to scour the forest for him next week and root him out. If you get news of him, 'twould be worth a silver mark here."

"Lord Sheriff," said Robin meekly, "if I can earn that silver mark, I will come back with the news. But I am a man of peace, and trust I do not fall in with this outlaw. I give you good day." Robin bowed and went out.

CHAPTER 4 / Little John's Quarter-Staff

WHEN Robin Hood had got back his own clothes from the potter, and handed over the horse and cart, he bade Will Scarlett lead his men back to their hiding place in the forest, and, taking his bow and the sword he had captured from Guy of Gisborne, set out alone for a look at his lands of Locksley. He reached them in mid-afternoon, to see that Guy's men were already sowing the barley he had hoped to sow, for spring was advancing fast now, and the trees had begun to put on their spring coats.

Again, as he watched and thought of the price set on his head, he renewed in his heart the promise he had made to Guy that the Abbot should pay in full for the farm, as should all fat abbots and great men who throve on the poverty of others. Henceforth the greenwood must be his home, he knew, and he could never go back to Locksley.

He turned back and made his way along a little track that would lead him to his band. This track took him down a wooded slope to a stream, across which a felled tree made a footbridge, and, as he neared the bridge from his side of the stream, a great, tall man came down to it from the other side. The tall man carried nothing but a big quarter-staff of oak, and he hurried, as did Robin, to be first to get to the bridge. Each of them set foot on it at the same time, and neither would draw back.

"Out!" said the giant. "Out, little man, and make

way for me, unless you want a ducking in the stream."

"Not so fast," said Robin, "or I will do the ducking myself, and leave you with a wet coat."

The great man swung his heavy quarter-staff within a foot of Robin's nose. "Get back!" he shouted, "before I hurt you."

But Robin, at the swing of the great staff, laid an arrow on his bowstring.

The giant dropped his staff and leaned on it as he stood on the bridge. "Now this is a coward facing me, for I have no bow," he said. "If I had, I could teach you how to shoot."

"No coward I," Robin retorted. "Had I such a staff as that, I would teach you more about quarter-play than you could ever teach me of archery."

"Go and cut a staff, then," said the giant, "for there are plenty about. I will wait here, and we will fight on the bridge. The one who thwacks the other into the stream shall have right to cross first."

Then with his hunting-knife Robin cut himself a great staff, trimmed it to his liking, and returned, at which the giant stood up and the fight began.

From the attitude of his opponent the giant could see that he had no easy task, and he began cautiously, feeling his way to find what Robin knew of quarter-staff play. He soon found out, for in less than a minute Robin gave him a thwack across the shoulders that shook him into rage, and after that they guarded and parried each other's blows till the great staves hummed, and the giant, skilfully evading the blows aimed at him, fairly danced on the bridge, until he nearly danced into the water.

"Keep at it, bantam," he roared, "the lesson is only just begun. Good guard, but I am only just warming to it. Look to your head!"

Parry and thrust and blow gave neither the advantage for a time, but then Robin caught the giant another mighty buffet which came down on his head and would have broken the skull of a weaker man.

"Take that," said Robin, "and let me across this bridge."

"Never," roared the big man, and, twirling his great staff, he came on again. Playing skilfully, in spite of the buzzing in his head after Robin's blow, he parried another like it and gave Robin a mighty thwack which made him lose his foothold and tumbled him into the stream with a great splash.

"Now," said the big man gleefully, "I cross the bridge first. But where are you gone?"

"Here, swimming with the stream," Robin answered from the water, as he caught at the log bridge and drew himself up. The giant leaned down and gave him a hand, roaring with laughter at his dripping figure. Then they sat down on the bridge together.

"Giant," said Robin, "never met I such a fighter with the staff. I yield you best at it."

" 'Twas a joyous fight," said the giant, "and I would I might meet such a fighter every day, but good men are scarce. We will have a match with the bow some day when I find you dry—but at a target, not at each other."

"Willingly," Robin answered. "But how do they call you, big man?"

"As a rule," said the giant, "they call me too late for a good meal, and so I am often hungry, but my name is John of Mansfield, since I come from that village."

"And what do you here in the forest?" Robin pursued.

"Hide," said John. "I was Ralph of Mansfield's man, and one morning I slept too late. Ralph is a cruel master, and he ordered me forty lashes for my sleep, but I took the whip and stunned the man that should have laid them on, and then there was naught for it but to flee."

"So!" said Robin. "Here is another Guy of Gisborne."

John laughed. "As like as a pea to another pea," he agreed. "They say that a man named Robin took Guy and tied him facing his horse's tail, and took to the forest after, being outlawed. I would put my hand in his and be his man," said John. "For look you, archer, I will give no man best with the quarter-staff, but a man may not earn his living by play alone, and this forest is an uneasy place if one have no companions."

"Put your hand in mine then," Robin said.

The giant stared at him.

"You—you are this Robin?" John asked, amazed.

Robin laughed. "And a-wanting good men," he answered. "Say, you tiny little man, how shall it be? Will you put your hand in mine and join with me now the chance is here?"

"Willingly, and now," said John. "Give me a good bow and feed me well, and I will draw a string with your best against Guy and his men."

"Then let us go, little John of Mansfield," Robin agreed, "for we have a full mile to trudge. And you being but a man and a half in size, we will name you Little John."

So they went on, and Robin's men gave their new comrade a good welcome when Robin had told them of the fight on the bridge and laughed at his own discomfiture at the game of quarter-staff. And this was one of the qualities that made him dear to his followers, that he could take a beating in good part.

There were then in Sherwood scores of masterless men like John of Mansfield, and when they heard how Robin had spoiled the Prior of Newark they sought him out with a view to joining him. But he would take only the best and most skilful at arms, and these he made to swear to follow the rules he had given to his nine men from Locksley. Even so, he had many more than nine when Guy of Gisborne came hunting him in Sherwood.

CHAPTER 5 / Guy of Gisborne's First Attempt

HALF-WAY between Ollerton and Worksop is a spot on which once stood the rich Abbey of St. Mary's, where Hugo de Rainault ruled in Robin Hood's time. A little to the north of it, on an eminence that commanded all the country round, rose the great castle of Belame, from which Isambart de Belame, as bad a baron as ever followed such a bad prince as John, terrorized the lands about him.

Isambart was useful to Abbot Hugo, so there was peace between them, no matter how Isambart outraged the people who fell into his grasp. And when Guy of Gisborne had been shamed and the Prior of Newark had suffered loss at Robin's hands, Abbot Hugo sent for Isambart to meet him and Guy, to make an end of the bold outlaw.

The three held a council in the Abbot's pleasant room in St. Mary's Abbey. Hugo was a great, fat man who always spoke Norman-French, though he understood English. Isambart was tall and lean and fierce, with a nose like a hawk's beak.

"It is ever the same," said the Abbot. "Let a man but get up and do some evil deed against us and the outlaws of the Forest will swarm round him. Now, as you know, Sir Isambart, we have few men-at-arms belonging to our Abbey."

"Some five or six less than you had before they tried to take this Robin of Locksley," Isambart agreed.

"And Guy, here, knows his way in Sherwood Forest," the Abbot pursued. "Now it is my wish that you lend me, say, thirty well-armed men to add to my own, and with Guy at their head they will root out this Robin before he becomes dangerous."

"And what do I get?" Isambart asked.

"You get the honour of helping Holy Church at need," said the Abbot.

Isambart smiled craftily. "A cheap reward," he remarked. "Good Hugo, since my wife died I am a lonely man in my castle of Belame. If I give you my help in this matter, you shall give me your ward Marian, who is under shelter at Kirklees with the Abbess there, but is none the less yours to give to any man."

"Ha!" said the Abbot. "This is a great reward you ask."

"Truly great," Isambart agreed, "for you thought to make a nun of Marian and take all her broad lands to add to yours of St. Mary's. But she is too beautiful to be a nun, and would better be wife to me."

"It is too much to ask," the Abbot said.

"So be it," Isambart replied, "but when this bold outlaw is burning your Abbey over your head you will wish you had paid the price of my thirty men before he set fire to you."

"Enough," said the Abbot hastily. "You shall have the maid when Guy here has done his work. It is a bargain."

"That is not the bargain," Isambart insisted. "If I lend you thirty of my men to follow Guy, then I shall have the maid whether he make an end of this Robin or no."

The Abbot reflected that with the score of men he

had himself, and Isambart's thirty, he would have a band that could easily put an end to a few ragged outlaws. It was safe enough.

"So be it, Sir Isambart," he said. "Give me the men to follow my steward on this hunt, and then Guy shall escort the maid Marian to your castle, to be married to you in the chapel there with him for witness."

"You shall have the men in three days," Isambart promised.

They held this council on the day that Robin sold pots in Nottingham, and Isambart kept his promise, so that thirty stout fellows, well armed, reported themselves to Guy of Gisborne outside his stone grange three days later. Then Guy gathered his men, and they set out for the depths of Sherwood.

They took two days' provisions with them, knowing that the hunt might be a long one. For Sherwood in those days was ten times the size it is now, a place of thickets and gloomy depths, and caves in which men might hide, and deep hollows.

Robin, who had explored the depths of the Forest from his boyhood, spied on the gathering at Guy's grange from a distance, and knew how many men Guy had with him, and he determined to lead them such a dance as had never been known in the Forest. He had now over thirty followers, all men that he had proved, and had no fear of Guy's band, who, heavily armed as they were, would soon tire on the tracks he meant them to follow.

When, a little after sunrise, Guy led his party from the grange, Robin himself and Little John lay up to watch them march. The two saw where the party would enter the forest, and Robin hurried to get on the track, where he laid a naked sword, with its point toward the way Guy and his men must come. Then he and Little John hid themselves.

Presently came Guy, fully armed and with his visor down, riding at the head of his men. He saw the sword lying on the grass, and bade one of his men pick it up. But, as the man stooped, a voice screeched out of the forest depths.

"Put that down! Dead men have no use for swords."

The man started back as if the sword had been a snake, frightened by the eldritch screech, which he took for the voice of one of the spirits of the forest.

"Pick it up, man!" Guy roared. "Art afraid of a voice?"

The man bent again to pick up the sword, and again the voice called out as he stooped.

"It is death to touch it—death to touch it!"

Again the man left the sword alone. "Master," he said, trembling, "I dare not. It is a fairy sword."

"You are a fairy fool!" Guy snorted. "Hold my horse."

In his full armour he started to dismount, to pick up the sword himself. Just as he lifted his leg over the high cantle of his saddle, a great arrow hummed out of the forest and rattled on the side of his helmet, so that he lost his balance and crashed to the ground like a crate of ironware. And then with yells his men took to their heels and bolted back, for the sword began to move of itself across the grass.

Guy, unharmed, got to his feet and, staring stupidly at the moving sword, saw that it was tied to a fine cord which led into the forest depths beside the track. He rushed at it, grasped, and snapped the cord.

"A trick—a trick!" he shouted. "Back here to me, you fools, and follow that cord! We will have the knave at the end!"

He ran into the thicket, not knowing that Robin had run the cord round a tree and back across the track to its other side, a little higher up. A dozen of Guy's men, recovering from their fear, followed their master; but they had nothing to guide them now, for Robin had pulled the cord out of their sight and wound it in.

As they beat the bushes with their swords, and thrust behind trees there came suddenly a screech of laughter from behind, an elfish noise that set them shuddering.

"Ha, ha, ha! Ha, ha, ha, ha, ha!" The voice echoed among the trees, so that they could not tell whence it came, nor who made it. Even Guy of Gisborne crossed himself in fear.

"It is the pixies of the wood," said one scared man to another. "Now we shall be led in circles till we drop and die of starvation, for once the pixies get at a man in Sherwood there is no escape for him."

"Silence, fool!" roared Guy. "It is but this pestilent outlaw tricking us. Let me but get on my horse and come at him and I will put an end to his tricks. Back to the path, and keep together."

He assembled the band again, all but two who, once they had started running, never stopped till they got back to St. Mary's grange, where they gave out that Guy of Gisborne and all his men were bewitched and lost in Sherwood depths, past any man's finding. But Guy led on along the track, and his men took heart and followed.

Now they came to a place where the track became very narrow between great trees, so that at one point they had all to go in single file. Guy himself went first on his horse, and his men followed on foot, one by one. The place was very gloomy because of the interlacing branches of the great trees over them. Here, as the last man waited his turn to move, a rope suddenly coiled down from the branches, with a loop at its end which tightened round his neck and drew him up, but not before he let out a wild yell of fear.

The men just in front, seeing him suddenly dangling in mid-air in the gloom, bolted forward, and it was a couple of minutes or more before any could come to his rescue. Then one of them ran and cut him down with a sword, and he tumbled on the grass, half strangled, and unable to speak for the time.

"Up that tree, one of you," Guy shouted, "and get me the villain who dropped the rope. Swift, before he escape!"

But all they found was the other end of the rope knotted round a branch, and no sign of any man. So far, except for this half-strangled man, they had come to no real harm, but every man of them devoutly wished himself out of this haunted forest.

And, in a glade a quarter of a mile away, Robin and his men were splitting their sides with laughter at the dance they were leading Guy's party, for this was sport after their own hearts.

"Now for the bridge," Robin said. "If they go on, they must come to the bridge. It is ready for them, eh, Will?"

"Ready and waiting, Robin," said Will Scarlett.

They went on through the forest to a point where two logs formed the main supports of a rough bridge across a stream, with smaller logs laid crosswise on them to make the roadway, and trampled brushwood on the cross pieces for footing. Here, again, Robin had had his men loop ropes round one end of each great log, and now they took their stand at the other ends of the two ropes, ten to each, well hidden in thickets. There they waited till Robin himself, on the watch for Guy's party, should give the word.

Marching solidly together, and searching every thicket on each side of the track, Guy and his men came down to the stream. The rough bridge was strong enough to take them all at once, and Guy rode down on to it, peering into the woods on the other side. He was half-way across, with a dozen of his men around him, when a voice called "Heave!"

Then Robin's two parties pulled on their ropes with all their force, and the two supporting logs of the bridge, with the earth dug away from their ends in readiness, parted, one upstream and one down, so that the bridge itself collapsed, and with a mighty splash Guy on his horse and his followers went into the depths of the stream. If it had not been for his horse, which pulled him ashore on the bank from which he had come, Guy of Gisborne would have been drowned in his heavy armour, and of his twelve followers one was drowned in the swift current before his fellows could rescue him. They had all they could do to scramble out themselves.

Now, while Guy stood shivering and cursing on the bank, with no bridge by which to cross, three men stepped into view on the far side of the stream. In the middle was Robin Hood with Little John on his right and Will Scarlett on his left.

"At them with your crossbows, you fools!" yelled Guy, soaked and wrathful. "There stands the outlaw himself—will you let him jeer at you in safety?"

"Hold!" Robin cried. "My men are all about you, and the first man who aims a bolt dies. So far, Guy of Gisborne, I and my men have but played with you. Go back to safety before we turn our play to earnest, if you would get out alive."

"Go back? Never!" shouted Guy. "Never till we have hanged you, rascal, and made an end of your tricks in Sherwood."

"Then look to yourselves," Robin answered. "We give you till nightfall to withdraw from the forest. If you are still within it then, it shall be at your peril."

"Shoot them down, men!" Guy shouted. "Here— give me a crossbow."

But before a bolt could be laid to string, the three had vanished, and there was the broad stream between their hiding-places and Guy of Gisborne's men. All the forest was silent and empty again, without a sign of enemy, though Guy and his men felt that they were watched by invisible eyes. So Guy thought better of it and led his men home.

And, after this, Robin had more offers of service in his band than he wanted, so that he was able to pick and choose only the very best of men to join his merry throng. It was in these days that his band grew to its strength of seven score great fighters, each of them a match for two ordinary men, and from then onward Robin was called the king of Sherwood.

CHAPTER 6 / Friar Tuck Joins the Band

In mid-morning one day Robin buckled on his sword, took his bow, and set out with Little John and Much. Noon had passed when they came up, hidden by the forest growth, to where a path led down toward a ford over a stream. On a little knoll beside the ford sat an enormous man in a friar's robe, which was tucked up into his belt. He gnawed at a great venison pasty, and down beside him stood a great flagon, the sight of which made all three of the outlaws feel thirsty.

"Do you two stay hidden here," Robin bade, "while I have a game with this great friar, who would be a good match for you, methinks, Little John."

He strode out toward the friar, who gave him one glance and then went on eating unconcernedly. Robin went straight up to him, suddenly whipped out his sword, and put the point of it at the friar's breast.

"Ho, you!" he said roughly. "Up and carry me across this stream, lest I wet my feet in the water."

The friar put down his half-eaten pasty and sighed. "Since it must be, it must be," he said. "Get up on my back then."

He bent his back, and Robin got on it, but took care to keep his drawn sword in his hand. The friar took to the water and waded in.

He splashed on, with the water nearly waist deep in the middle of the ford, and came out on the other bank. Then, as Robin slipped from his back, the friar

43

turned and gripped him with surprising agility, snatched away his sword, and flung him down on the turf.

"My turn to ride!" he said. "Up, man, and carry me back to my dinner, else I will spit you on this skewer of yours!"

There was no help for it, Robin knew—his own trick had been turned against him. He bent his back, and the friar, getting up on it, made him grunt with his great weight.

But when they got to the bank again, and the friar got down ponderously, Robin suddenly bent himself and jumped backward, hitting the friar in a way that knocked all the wind out of him and caused him to drop the sword. With a nimble leap Robin picked it up.

"No dinner yet, friar," he said. "Carry me back, and be careful over it, or I'll slice an ear off you."

Again the friar took to the water, with Robin on his back, and waded in; when he had got to the middle he suddenly bent nearly double and pitched Robin into the stream.

"Now, impudent rascal, sink or swim," he said. "I am for my dinner."

And back he went, leaving Robin to climb out from the water, laughing at the adventure. Presently Robin came up to him, with his sword in its sheath, all dripping from the water.

"A bold monk this," said Robin. "Tell me your name."

"Men call me Friar Tuck. How do they call you, rascal?"

"Robin of Locksley, but better known as Robin Hood."

The friar leaped to his feet with a laugh. "What?" he asked. "Have I made carry me the man who sent Guy of Gisborne home in his shirt and spoiled the Prior of Newark?"

"So," said Robin, "but I made you carry me too. Now, friar, there is more meat like that you are eating in Sherwood, and many a drink like that in your flask. I have come out to-day to find you."

"Here is a man who likes priors and abbots as little as I like them myself," said the friar, "and has as little respect for the king's deer as I have. But perhaps, Robin, you keep fast days in Sherwood. Is it so?"

"If you will join my band, we will keep just as many fast days as you order us," Robin promised.

"Ah, tempt me not, Robin Hood—tempt me not! For I am a holy man."

"Venison, friar—good fat deer, well cooked, a roast swan once in a while, and pheasants. Strong ale a-plenty, and good casks of wine as well. Come with us, for we need such a cook as I have heard you are."

"Enough, Robin—I yield," the friar said with a chuckle. "It is too much for sinful man to resist."

"Now we shall have a chaplain to our band," Robin remarked, and raised his hand in a signal, at which Scarlett and Little John came out of the wood toward their chief. Friar Tuck stared at the mighty form of Little John and sighed.

"Good Robin," he said, "if you keep such tiny babies in your band as this we must e'en take back some feeding bottles."

"If it were not for your robe and cowl, friar," said Little John, "I would cut me a quarter-staff and tan your hide."

"Cut it, man, and I will throw back the cowl and tuck up the robe," the friar offered. "For so they call me Friar Tuck, since ever my robe is tucked in my belt to let me fight more freely. Let us have a bout, and I will warrant you cry for mercy."

"We will have that bout in our glade, not here," said Robin. "Let us away, friar, if you are ready."

So Robin Hood won Friar Tuck to join his band, and they say there was no merrier or braver man than the good friar in all the Midlands. He could sing them a song, cook them a royal feast, and fight well at need.

CHAPTER 7 / How Robin Won the Silver Arrow

Now that Robin had got his band together little passed in the North Midlands, or in Yorkshire itself, of which he did not know, for the country people, seeing that he was for their rights and against the oppression of the barons and the church dignitaries, gave him and his men any aid they asked. This was the time when John ruled England in his brother's absence, and Queen Berengaria, together with the Queen-Mother, Eleanor, laid all England under heavy tribute to get together the money to ransom King Richard, who lay a prisoner to Luitpold of Austria in the castle of Gratz.

Even John himself, much as he feared his brother's return, helped to gather in tribute for the ransom, and for that purpose made a progress of the midland counties. When he came to Nottingham, the Sheriff, Robert de Rainault, held a tournament in his honour, for Robert was John's man and profited by John's tyrannies. Much, the miller's son, who had been to visit his father, brought back news of the tournament.

"There will be rare sport on the third day," said Much, "for there is to be archery at a mark, after the sword-play on foot, and the prize for the best archer is a silver bugle and a silver arrow feathered.with gold."

"I have a mind to hang that bugle over my

shoulder and to put the silver arrow in my quiver," said Robin Hood thoughtfully.

"There is too much risk in it, good master," Little John warned him. "Many a man in Nottingham would be glad of the forty gold marks the Sheriff set as the price of your head."

"And many a man there would guard me from the Sheriff," said Robin. "Little John, we will go after that bugle and the arrow. Out of all the clothes and armour we have taken of late, there will be disguises for a couple of score of us, and I will shoot for the Sheriff's prize."

They planned it out, decided who should go to Nottingham to see Robin shoot for the Sheriff's prize, and how they should disguise themselves.

When the day came, there arrived at Pike's field certain millers, dusty with the meal and flour of their trade, and cattle herders with smocks and hats pulled down over their eyes, and a giant beggar who limped on a crutch, as Little John had decided that was his best disguise, and all these watched the sword play and cheered the winners most lustily.

Although it was the third day of the tournament there was a brilliant gathering of knights and their ladies up in the stand with Count John and the Sheriff, and the field was thronged with sightseers from miles round, for seldom did such great people come to Nottingham. When the swordsmen had finished and the targets were set up for archery, the people flocked to the barriers on either side to see the shooting, as nearly sixty tall fellows stood forth to shoot.

Among them was an old, ragged man with dirty face and torn cap.

Now Prince John, seeing this ragged ancient among so many stout fellows, leaned forward in his seat and called down to the lists.

"Clerk," he asked harshly, "what does that ragged beggar among the archers? Why is he there?"

"Sire," the clerk called back, "he enters himself to shoot against them for the silver bugle and arrow."

There was a ripple of laughter among the crowd, but the old man shook his fist at the clerk and turned to the royal stand.

"Your worship," he squeaked, "I be Hodden o' Barnsdale, and as good a man as these beef-fed louts, any day."

"Turn him out, clerk," cried the Sheriff.

"Not so," said John, "let the man shoot. And if he put not an arrow in the target he shall be drubbed out of the lists."

Now the archers were lined up, six at a time, for the first trial, which would leave one man in every six to shoot off for the prize. When Hodden o' Barnsdale's turn came, he was three inches nearer the centre of the target than any other of his six.

"Chance, mere chance," said the clerk angrily, for he had hoped to see old Hodden beaten.

There were now twelve men left. Old Hodden had shot best; but it was regarded as a chance shot. Now a single great target was set up, into which each man of the dozen must shoot an arrow in turn till each had shot three arrows, but if any man missed the target altogether he must retire from the contest. The distance was one hundred and twenty yards.

The first two archers missed altogether, and walked off with mortification on their faces. Then came Hubert, who landed his shaft within six inches of the black spot in the centre of the target, and two more who only scored on the outer edge. Then old Hodden, stepping into place with a grin, loosed off a shaft so carelessly that he seemed to take no aim at all, and turned away before the arrow struck the target.

"Child's play this," he said.

But from the watchers near the target a roar went up, for his arrow was in the black spot, barely half an inch across.

Then another roar went up, for Henry, John's archer, had planted a shaft within an eighth of an inch of old Hodden's.

No other archer came near the centre of the target in this first round, and, since three more missed altogether, there were but seven left for the second stage of the contest. Old Hodden, having made the best shot before, was set to shoot first when the fresh target was put up, and he loosed off his arrow with as little care as before.

"They should set up a mark to make it worth a man's while to try," he said as he turned away. "Shooting at that great white thing is no more than throwing stones in a pond."

And down at the other end of the range the spectators yelled and threw up their hats. "A Hodden—a Hodden!" they cried, for the old man had put his arrow in the black spot again. But when John's man Henry had shot they went wild, for Henry split Hodden's arrow with his shot.

"Man," said Hodden to Henry, "there are few archers like us two, and be he Norman or English, I love a man who can put in such a shaft as that."

Henry regarded the old man curiously. "I would take a lesson or two off you, Master Hodden," he answered, "for mine is my best shooting, while with you it is a matter of ease."

"Later maybe," Hodden said. "Let us see what this braggart of the Sheriff's choosing will do."

But Hubert cursed when he saw that his shaft was a good two inches off the spot, though he had dwelt long on his aim. Still, he cheered up when two more of the seven missed this smaller target, and left only five for the final shot, with only Hodden and Henry better than himself.

Now the clerk, turning towards where John sat, called out the names of the five left in, and John signed to him.

"Bring them before us, clerk," he called.

So the five were ranged before the stand, with Henry on the right, and Hodden o' Barnsdale next to him. John nodded at his man. "Go to it, Henry," he bade, "and when I hand you the bugle I will see that it is filled with silver pennies."

"Your worship," old Hodden squeaked, "he hath yet to win the prize. When I have beaten him, will the bugle be filled wi' silver pennies for me?"

"Ha! You beat Henry?" John mocked. "Aye, if you can beat such an archer I will fill the bugle with silver pennies."

"Thank ye, your worship. Since a Norman thief stole my land my old woman ha' wanted a new gown, and the pennies 'ull buy her a rare one."

"Aye," said John, angered again, "and you who dare call Normans thieves to our face shall have your right hand cut off when Henry has beaten you and

taken the bugle. Away with them to their work, clerk, and watch this old rascal closely, lest he run away after his shot."

The five were ranged up before a still smaller target, and Hubert was first to shoot. He missed the black spot in the centre by a bare half inch and stood back with a frown of vexation. Then old Hodden raised another cheer as he planted his arrow in the black, but not exactly in the centre. Then came Henry, whose arrow struck level with old Hodden's in the black, so that the two shots were exactly equal. The other two made worse shots than Hubert, and retired.

"Your worship," said the clerk to the Sheriff, "Henry and Hodden o' Barnsdale must shoot it off, for they have tied."

Henry stood forward, dwelt long on his aim and shot. There was a buzz of applause, for his arrow landed in the black, though well to the left.

"Now, old fool!" John cried, excited over his man's shooting, "take your stand and loose your last arrow, before you lose your hand."

With no sign of fear, Hodden stepped to his place and this time, it was noted, he took more careful aim. The great arrow hummed from the string and struck with a thud, and again the crowd roared applause, for Hodden's shot had split Henry's arrow, and landed in the centre of the black.

"Your worship," said old Hodden, "this shooting at walls o' white is but a game for babes. Let us set up a peeled willow wand at a hundred and fifty cloth yards, and the first to split it takes the bugle."

"Why then, you old fool," said John, "We shall sit

here till Christmas and longer, for no man ever hit such a target."

"Lord," said Henry, "I have heard of such shooting, and once I have hit such a target, though but at fifty yards. If the old man is willing, then so am I."

"So be it," said John. "One shot apiece, and he who shoots nearest to the wand shall take the bugle and the silver arrow."

The last target was cleared away; a slip of willow peeled and stuck in the ground, and the distance carefully measured off.

"Do you shoot first," Hodden said to his opponent, "for there are clouds coming, and I would give you the best light."

"Master," said Henry, "you be a right courteous old man, and I thank you. But no man can hit the wand at that distance, and we must find another mark when we have failed at this."

He made a good attempt, dwelling long on his aim, and twice lowering his bow at the merest breath of wind. At last he shot, and a great "Ooh!" of wonder went up from the watchers, for his arrow had grazed the wand.

"A fine shot, good Henry," said old Hodden, as he stooped and plucked a spike of grass. He threw it in the air, to get the set of the faint breeze, twanged his bowstring, and set the arrow on it. Then he stepped to the mark, took careful aim, and let fly. A mighty shout went up when it was seen that he had split the wand fairly with the arrow.

Old Hodden turned to Henry and held out his hand. "Though the bugle is mine, do you take the pennies out of it, Master Henry," he said, "for I would not wish to shoot against a better man."

But Henry shook his head. "I have pennies a-plenty, old man," he answered, "and the full prize is yours, fairly won. Do you take it all, and may we yet meet for another match."

"I trust so," said Hodden. "I will go and claim my prize."

So he went up to where John, very unwillingly, held the silver bugle full of pennies in one hand, and the beautiful gold and silver arrow in the other. John frowned at him fiercely.

"Old man," he said, "I would I had had that right hand of yours lopped off rather than you should take this prize. Take it and begone."

"For such courtesy, your worship, no less than for the prize, my thanks," Hodden answered, and took the bugle and the arrow. With a quick movement he swung the bugle, flinging its contents of silver pennies far and wide among the people who stood round to watch, and then he backed away from where John and the Sheriff sat.

"Stop—hold that man!" John cried. "'Tis some thief disguised, for such as he seems do not fling silver pennies away."

But Hodden was already clear of the crowd about the stand, and, with an arrow ready on his string, he pointed straight at John's craven heart.

"Take back that order, or die, Count John!" he cried in ringing tones.

"Let him go—let him go!" John yelled, in sheer terror.

Now Guy of Gisborne, who had watched the

shooting, and more especially had kept an eye on old Hodden, suddenly reached out and grasped the archer's tattered old hat. It came off, and with it the dirty old grey wig and beard that had concealed his face.

" 'Tis Robin Hood—seize him!" Guy shouted. "Outlawed—forty marks for the man who takes him——"

But he said no more, for just then the limping beggar raised his crutch and brought it down on Guy's head with such force that he dropped senseless, and Little John's voice roared out:

"A Hood! A Hood! To us, merry men, English all!"

A score or more of stout fellows, armed with great quarter-staves, came knocking their way through the crowd that gathered round, and Robin, seizing a staff, retreated with them after he had slung his bow so as to have both hands free. Meanwhile Little John's shout had served its purpose of setting the Saxon English people of Nottingham against John's Norman followers, and in five minutes or less there were a dozen separate fights going on, while John and the Sheriff fled for safety, and Robin and his men retreated steadily beyond the barriers of the lists.

Here they came on a body of men-at-arms, set to keep order among the crowd, and now drawn up with swords ready to stop them. But Robin and Little John advanced with a rush, with quarter-staves whizzing round them, and the first who tried conclusions with them found their swords either shattered or whirled out of their hands by the flying staves. And when Will Scarlett, Much, and the rest of the band joined issue with the men-at-arms, and the staves rattled on their pates in earnest, such as were not laid stunned took to their heels and bolted, while the good people of Nottingham roared with laughter to see John's hated followers put to flight in such fashion.

Without the loss of a man, Robin drew off, and the surging crowds prevented any men whom the Sheriff sent in pursuit from finding which way he had gone. The outlaws reached the shelter of the forest in safety, and made their way to their retreat.

"'Twas a joyous adventure, Robin," said Little John, as they ate, "but we will not go to Nottingham again this month."

CHAPTER 8 / The Rescue
of Maid Marian

ABOUT a fortnight after the tournament at Nottingham, Isambart de Belame came to Hugo de Rainault, Abbot of St. Mary's. Hugo welcomed his ally in his own comfortable room in the Abbey, sent for a flagon of his best wine, and settled to hear what Isambart had to say.

"The summer is passing," said Isambart, "and I would get married before the crops are gathered, Abbot Hugo."

"A wise resolve," Hugo agreed, nodding. "So you come to me for a priest to marry you in the chapel of Belame?"

"A priest, yes," said Isambart, "and the bride as well, according to our bargain when I lent you thirty of my men to root out the outlaws from Sherwood Forest."

"Surely, man," the Abbot protested, "you would not claim that bargain?"

"A bargain is a bargain," Isambart retorted.

"Let us talk it over. You say you would wed the maid."

"That was the bargain."

"Ha! Hum!" Hugo reflected awhile, for he could not afford to break his friendship with Isambart. "Well," he said when he had thought it out, "the maid has no taste to be a nun, and she must marry somebody. I will send to Kirklees and bid her prepare to marry you."

"When?" Isambart asked, rather grimly.

"I will send a man to-morrow," the Abbot promised.

"Now look you, Abbot," said Isambart, "this is no matter for shifts and tricks. Send your steward, Guy of Gisborne, with an escort of a dozen good men, and have the maid convoyed safely to my castle of Belame within the week. Send me, too, a priest to marry us, and the bargain will then be kept. Shall it be so?"

Hugo nodded assent, reluctantly, for there was no way out of it that he could see. When Isambart had gone he sent for Guy of Gisborne and explained what must be done.

"So you take the men, Guy, and set out to-morrow," he bade. "Have them all well mounted, and ride to Kirklees for the maid. And see that you go well armed, and keep clear of Robin Hood and his men till the maid is safely at the castle."

Guy went out to do the Abbot's bidding.

Next day came a wandering beggar into Robin Hood's retreat in Sherwood, one of the scouts who brought in news every day to the outlaws' hold, and he told how Guy of Gisborne and his men were setting out to escort Marian from Kirklees.

"Aye," said Robin, "but where do they take her? Not to the Abbey, surely, for that is no place for her?"

"They take her to Castle Belame, to be married to Isambart."

"What?" Robin shouted. "Marry a fair maid to that thieving wolf? I say this shall not be. One wife of Isambart's has pined to death in Evil Hold, and there shall be no more while I rule in Sherwood. Let us arm a couple of score of the band with the good armour we took from Guy of Gisborne and his men, and ambush him on his way to Isambart's castle."

And so it was done. Robin sent out spies to find out the road by which Guy of Gisborne would travel to Evil Hold, and, when the time came, set out with his men and lay up in a thicket beside the track, a little beyond Worksop. They had waited half a morning, and began to fear that Guy had taken some other road, when Robin spied a couple of armed men riding down from the Yorkshire border, and there was talk and the clatter of hoofs behind them. When they were still a score yards away he stood out alone in the middle of the track, and saw Guy, heavily armed, leading a white palfrey on which rode the maid he had been sent to find at Kirklees and escort to Isambart.

With arrow on the string, Robin stood, and the two foremost men reined in at sight of him.

"Stand, Guy of Gisborne!" Robin cried. "Deliver up the maid for escort back to Kirklees, and I will do you no harm."

They say that Marian, seeing him standing there, one man defying a score, loved him from that minute. For the journey had been a thing of dread for her, and she loathed the thought of going to Evil Hold, yet could see no way of escape, since she was Hugo's ward and must do his bidding. But Guy pointed at the lone figure with a yell.

"Robin Hood—seize him, men! Fifty gold marks wait for the man who takes him! At him, you villains!"

Now fifty gold marks, in those days, would buy a

farm and leave some over, so Guy's men needed no second bidding. The two foremost spurred at him, one a little in front of his fellow, and Robin's arrow crashed into the brain of the leading horse, which, falling to earth lay in the track so that the second rider came to grief. The two of them lay stunned and helpless, one pinned down by the dead horse and the other kicked by his floundering steed before it got up and galloped away.

"Must I be always baulked by this rascally hound?" Guy roared in rage. "At him, you others, and seize the outlaw!"

But not one of them moved to obey, for Robin had another arrow on the string, and they knew since the tournament at Nottingham that he never missed. With a curse, Guy dropped the palfrey's rein, drew his sword, and spurred at the lone figure just as Robin raised his silver bugle and blew a blast on it. Suddenly the woods became alive with armed men, surrounding the maid and Guy's followers, while Robin stepped aside as his enemy thundered past, and stooped to evade the sword.

"Foul stroke, Guy," he said, as Guy tried to rein in and come back at him. "Get down, man, and let us have it out."

But Guy looked back and saw that his men were all being disarmed and pinioned by Robin's followers, who outnumbered his party by two to one and more. He struck in his spurs and galloped on, leaving Marian to her fate.

Robin watched the fleeing man for perhaps a hundred yards, and then lifted his bow. The heavy arrow sang on its way and took the horse behind his

shoulder, so that he came down with a mighty crash, and Guy lay in his armour on the track. Robin strode up to him and prodded him with his foot, laughing.

"Why, man," he said, "this is a poor sort of escort. To leave a maid in distress, in the hands of savage outlaws, is no sort of play for an honest steward. How will it sound in the ears of Abbot Hugo when he hears?"

Guy scrambled to his feet. "Mocker and thief!" he said fiercely, "if I had but my sword you should mock no more."

Robin pointed to where the sword had fallen. "Take the sword," he said, "and though you be in armour and I but clad for the woods, we will try a bout here and now, Steward. For surely you will strike a blow for the maid you were to guard?"

The game was up, Guy knew. He could not hope to get Marian out of the clutches of Robin and his men, and, with his horse lying dead, there was no chance of flight.

"And if I beat you," he said sullenly, "your men will but kill me."

"Now, now!" Robin protested, "that is the way of a Norman cur, I know well, but it is not the way of us of the greenwood. Should you beat me, Guy of Gisborne, you go free to your master, but the maid shall not go to Isambart in Evil Hold. So take your sword, and let us see if your work with it is as big as your bragging."

Without more ado Guy took up his sword, and found Robin ready when he turned to stand on guard. They went at their grim work with a will, and the flashing blades ground on each other as they thrust and parried, while Robin's men, having disarmed and tied up Guy's followers, came round to watch the duel, and Marian urged the palfrey forward with a prayer for the safety of her deliverer.

For ten minutes or more, the blades flashed in the sunlight, and Guy panted in his armour, striving with every trick he knew to get past Robin's guard; but in vain. By the end of that time it was apparent that Robin was merely playing with his opponent, dancing round him and fencing lightly with a smile on his lips.

"Now steady, Guy," he bade mockingly. "Save breath, man—save breath! If the Abbot have no better swordsmen than you, his Abbey is poorly guarded. Bad thrust—try again!"

A little ripple of laughter went up from the watchers, which infuriated Guy. He made a couple of wild passes that Robin parried easily, and then with a twist so quick that no man could tell quite how it was done Robin ripped his sword out of his grasp and sent it flying into the bushes.

"Now, steward," he said, lowering his own point, "what shall we do with you? We have already one suit of your armour, and it would be a pity to spoil you of this you wear."

"Mock me no more," said Guy sullenly, "but kill me and make an end."

"This is no day for killing," Robin answered. "Get you gone to Abbot Hugo and tell him the maid is in safe keeping on her way back to Kirklees. Tell him, too, that if Isambart press his suit any more, I will come and burn Evil Hold."

"You mean to let me go?" Guy asked incredulously.

"Why should I keep you?" Robin answered. "It would but be wasting the food that a good man might eat, and we in Sherwood do not hunt the deer to feed such as you."

He turned and beckoned to Little John. "Turn these men of his loose, each with his hands so tied behind his back that they cannot untie each other," he said. "And tie Guy's hands too, and put him on a horse, for he is tired after that bout with the sword. Now do you, Guy, ride with these men where you will, so long as you ride away from here, and see that you do not come against me again, or I may not treat you so easily next time."

When Little John and the rest had done his bidding, Robin watched Guy and his sorry band of followers ride off toward St. Mary's Abbey. Then he turned to Marian, who still sat waiting on the white palfrey.

She was slim and fair, the chroniclers tell, with great blue eyes and hair of gold, a right fair maid, who, at her father's death, had been given into the wardship of Abbot Hugo till she should come of age and marry with his approval. Robin made her a low bow.

"We have saved you from the clutch of Isambart de Belame," he said, "and now, if you will, we will escort you back to safety at Kirklees."

"Good sir," she answered, "I have no wish to go back to Kirklees, for if I did I should still be at the mercy of Abbot Hugo, who perhaps would yet find a way to send me to the fiend who rules in Evil Hold."

"Why, that is true," said Robin, "yet a fair maid like you cannot wander about the world with nobody to guard and shelter you, and all your lands and wealth are in Hugo's clutches, I know. Where can you go, if not to Kirklees?"

Marian looked down and blushed. "I am among loyal, honest men, I see, in spite of the tales I have heard of Robin Hood and his men. May I not remain among them?"

Robin came near and looked into her eyes.

"It would give us all great joy to have such a one among us," he told her, "yet the greenwood is no place for maidens who have been used to shelter and every care. 'Tis but a rough life we live in the forest glades, and you would weary of it."

"Good Robin," she answered, "I had sooner have my freedom among good men, and go in rags, than live in luxury and know fear of those round me. Find me shelter, and when I come to my inheritance I will repay."

"Nay, now," Robin said, "there is no question of repayment. What say you, Little John, shall we give her her will, and take such a fair flower as this to the shelter of the forest?"

Marian turned to Little John. "Good giant," she said, "plead for me with your chief. I have great knowledge of medicines and the art of healing, and I can cook and sew."

"Well, Robin," said Little John, "there is Will Scarlett's wife for company for her, and if, as she say, she have knowledge of medicines, she may find something that will sweeten Dame Scarlett's tongue, for it is bitter enough, and so poor Will may have an easier time."

"Think what it would have been for me if I had been taken to Evil Hold, good Robin Hood," Marian urged. "Is life in the greenwood any worse than such a fate as that?"

"If it were," Robin answered, "I would go and beg

the Sheriff of Nottingham to hang me out of hand. I see no choice, Marian, for, as you say, if we take you back to Kirklees, Isambart will get you sooner or later, and there is no other place that would hold you when Abbot Hugo bade that you be given up. But it is a poor fate for such a maid as you."

She looked down at him. "It is such a fate as I would ask," she said, "and I will come and be one of your band gladly. Now let us go on, lest Guy of Gisborne rouse up more men."

Robin laughed. "If Guy's fighting is all we are likely to suffer from," he said, "life will be an easy business. You shall come and be Queen of Sherwood, Marian—how say you, men? Will she not make a fair queen to rule over our band?"

Little John flung his hat in the air. "Here is a joyous adventure!" he cried. "Three cheers, all of you, for the Queen!"

They roared their cheers so lustily that Abbot Hugo might have heard them at St. Mary's had he been listening. Robin reached up and grasped Marian's hand.

"Remember," he said, "that there is a king in Sherwood too, Marian. Would you be queen to me as well as Sherwood?"

"Right gladly," she answered, "for I have seen no such man as you in all my life, and I owe you freedom and everything else from to-day."

Robin gave the word to move, and they set out on their way back to the forest hold. As they went Little John came up beside his leader, who walked by the white palfrey talking to Marian.

"Robin," said Little John, " 'Twas a lucky chance that sent you to win our friar to the band, for now he can do the marrying between you two, and we shall have no need to borrow a priest from St. Mary's."

"True," said Robin, "and we will make a feast day of it, and set the good friar to cooking after he has made us two man and wife."

So it was done, and they say that there was no such fair and loving wife in all the Midlands as was Maid Marian to Robin Hood. And, though he knew that he had made a bitter enemy of Isambart de Belame by this rescue, Robin slept none the worse.

Isambart took no action for the time. But he waited for revenge all the same.

CHAPTER 9 / How the Sheriff Took a Hand

THE Sheriff put no faith in the reports that Robin had over a hundred men in the forest, for never had he been seen anywhere with more than thirty or forty. A body of eighty stout fellows, with himself at the head, Robert reflected, would clear Sherwood of outlaws, and he called up that number to go hunting Robin Hood and his men.

The Sheriff, warned by what had happened to Guy of Gisborne, divided his men into two parties, putting forty under his man Hubert, and leading the rest himself. Hubert went straight into the forest from Nottingham, while the Sheriff took his forty up as far as Locksley farm, on the Abbot's lands, to drive into Sherwood from there. He had arranged with Hubert that they should meet at Dark Mere, a great pool in the depths of Sherwood, and trusted that by having two parties march in from different points they would come across some of Robin Hood's men.

The day was hot, and the Sheriff's men sweated in their armour as they beat and searched the thickets of the forest, but all in vain. Sharp eyes kept watch on them at their work, but it was one thing to enter Sherwood and another to find men in it, and not a man did they see the whole day long, except for a couple of ragged charcoal burners who denied any knowledge of Robin Hood and his band, though rags and a black face disguised Much the miller's son, and

Will Scarlett, if only the Sheriff had known it. He questioned the two himself.

"I have heard," said Much doubtfully, "that the rogue hath got wind of your worship's search for him, and hath gone up into Yorkshire to escape from you. It was a great fat friar who told me."

"A great fat friar?" Robert de Rainault questioned. "Why, if he were alone in Sherwood that will be their Friar Tuck, one of this Robin Hood's band. Which way went the friar?"

"He was headed north, and said he was for Yorkshire too," said this deceitful charcoal burner. "But of course, your worship, he may have been lying, as fat friars will at times."

"Aye, and lean ones too," the Sheriff agreed. "Look you, fellow, my bands meet this night at Dark Mere, and if you get any news of this Robin Hood's men and bring it to me there, I will have a silver mark ready for you."

With that he bade his men march on and leave the two charcoal burners to their work. As soon as the last man was out of sight, Much and Scarlett went through the denser part of the forest to where Robin lay hidden with about fifty of his band. Much reported his talk with the Sheriff, and Robin and Little John laughed over it.

"Let them search," said Robin, "till they are all tired men. Robert de Rainault is a bigger fool than I took him to be, else he had not come into Sherwood with so few men. We will be at Dark Mere to-night too."

"Much, you rascal," said Friar Tuck, "did you dare tell the Sheriff it was a great fat friar?"

Much nodded. "I told him so," he answered.

"An you dare to call me fat, I shall be tempted to forget my sacred self and baste you with my quarterstaff," Friar Tuck objected. "Great, maybe, for I am no common man, but not fat, Much. It is all good brawn and muscle about me, as you will know if I have cause to give you a buffet over this."

"Well, friar," said Much, "we may as well have a game of buffets while the Sheriff gets on with his hunting."

"Stand to it," the friar offered. "Do you buffet first."

He stood up and braced himself for the blow. Much gave him a tremendous cuff with his hand, and the friar rocked a little on his feet, but no more. He nodded in a satisfied way.

"Not bad for a growing lad, Much," he said. "Now it is my turn."

So Much braced himself for the blow, and Friar Tuck drew back his robe from his great arm, took a long breath, and struck. The blow fell with a resounding smack, and sent Much full length on the grass, where he lay while the friar and the rest of them gazed down at him.

"'Twas but a little pat, good Much," said Friar Tuck contentedly. "Now if I had really struck you, you would still be spinning. But call me not fat next time you talk of me."

"Now let us two try a round," Little John said to the friar.

"Not now," Robin Hood said, "for Hubert and his men will come this way in a matter of minutes. To the trees, all of you, till they are gone, they must find the forest empty to-day."

Empty enough it was when Hubert and his band

came by, though scores of pairs of eyes watched them pass. It was within an hour of sunset then, and the Sheriff's men were grumbling as they went about their task.

" 'Tis a crime to put us few to such work," said one.

"Aye," said another, "for it would take an army to search the whole of Sherwood. We shall be weeks at this game, unless the Sheriff grow tired of it, and I know we are on the wrong track. Robin Hood's hold is far over to the west from here, a couple of miles or more beyond Dark Mere."

"That man knows too much," said Robin Hood, who could hear plainly all that was said. "It is time to hasten to our rendezvous. We should all be placed and ready for our game with the Sheriff before it grows dark."

When Hubert and his party got to Dark Mere, they found the Sheriff already there with his forty men, in a thoroughly bad temper over their wasted day. They had brought food with them, and they ate, and made their bivouac after sentries had been posted, by which time the twilight was almost gone, and the gloom under the great trees deepened mysteriously. As superstitious as were most men in those days, the Sheriff's men gazed into the shadows with fear of bogles and sprites and demons, and told each other tales of the evil things that haunted the forest depths.

"Men say a dragon used to lurk in this mere," said one.

"And you call to mind the tale of the smith of Barnsdale, who came this way," said another. "The fairies took him and led him round and round a tree all night, and in the morning he was so cross-eyed that you could never tell which way he was looking."

"Aye," said a third, "and the poor man was dumb from that day on, and so could never tell what had happened to him."

"How did folk know what had happened to him then?" asked a listener.

But reply was prevented by a burst of demon laughter, which seemed to come from all points at once, and echoed through the forest glades.

They stared, pale with fright, but saw nothing. Robin had determined to play on their fears and prevent them from getting any rest, and had set his men to laugh from different points. Now the Sheriff, who conquered his fears of the evil things of the forest, took ten men and went to look for the cause of the laughter, but, of course, he found nothing.

"There is nothing to fear, men," he said when he came back—though he did not believe it himself. "It is these outlaws who try to trick us as they did Guy of Gisborne and his men. But they dare not attack us —we are too strong for them."

Again the demon laughter echoed round them, shrill and long and mocking. Even the Sheriff's teeth began to chatter, in spite of his words, while his men shrunk close to each other and drew their swords, peering into the darkness round them with frightened eyes.

" 'Tis no man's laugh, that," said one. " 'Tis bogles."

The Sheriff made the sign of the cross and wished he had brought a priest with the party. He thought of his good warm bed in Nottingham and wished himself safe in it.

Again and again the ghostly laughter sounded round them, seeming to come from every point at once. The Sheriff had posted eight sentries round their bivouac, and he could just see them standing in the darkness. While they were there to give the alarm in case of attack, he felt there was no real danger, for he was confident that Robin Hood had no more than forty men in his band altogether.

The night wore on with his men shivering in dread of what the forest might hold, with the terrible laughter echoing round them ever and again, never in any definite direction. When the Sheriff wanted to go out and search again, his men refused to budge from each others' company, and he was forced to give up.

About two hours after dark he went out to change his sentries, and found that what he had taken for the men standing at their posts were straw dummies propped up with sticks. The eight sentries had vanished, silently and mysteriously, and though the badly frightened Sheriff called out for them till he was hoarse there was no reply, except for the bursts of horrible laughter that sounded at intervals.

IT was worse than useless for the Sheriff to attempt
to post more sentries, for the men were too frightened to leave their main body now, and de Rainault
could only order the whole force to stand to arms for
the rest of the night.

Silence came about them, deep and unbroken, until midnight, and they waited for dawn to give them
a chance of searching for their lost companions.
They were beginning to doze in the stillness when
one of them caught sight of a flying form down by
the waters of Dark Mere, and he cried out and
pointed. A second figure followed the first, then a
third, running out of one patch of shadows into
another, and then came a fourth, and a fifth, all running silently as if they had been ghosts. The Sheriff's
hair bristled with dread, but he conquered his
feelings.

"The outlaws at last, men!" he said. "Up and after
them."

With drawn sword, he ran down to where the five
figures had disappeared, and his man Hubert followed, also with drawn sword. But, for a minute or
more, not a man of the band moved, and then they
went down toward the Mere irresolutely, ashamed of
their cowardice. But it was too late, for both the
Sheriff and Hubert had vanished as if the earth had
swallowed them.

Robin and his men, waiting in the gloom, had

served them as they had served the sentries. A heavy cloth flung over the head of each, and a swift blow had stunned them before they could cry out, and then Robin's men bore them away, each with a gag thrust into his mouth lest he should recover enough to shout for help. In that state they were carried all the way to the secret glade where the outlaws made their head-quarters, while the band that the Sheriff had brought into the forest with him waited helplessly.

When morning came they held counsel among themselves, some arguing that they ought to stay where they were till the Sheriff reappeared to lead them, others that they ought to go and search for him, and yet others declaring that they would look for no man in this haunted forest.

"The dragon of the mere hath got them all," declared one.

"No dragon, but the bogles of the wood," said another.

" 'Twas plain, simple enchantment," said the first, "if it were not the dragon. I doubt me we shall be led to walk this forest for ever in mazed circles, being enchanted too, or else we shall all be turned into trees or wild hogs by the demon."

They wrangled and argued among themselves for awhile longer, and decided that, as they had seen no sign of Robin Hood or any of his men, and it was useless to search for Robert de Rainault, they had better go back to Nottingham.

So back they went, weary and ashamed after their day of tramping through the forest and the sleepless night of terror that had followed. They found no sign of the Sheriff anywhere, and, when they told how he had disappeared, Dame de Rainault called them cowards who had deserted her husband.

While Nottingham buzzed with excitement, the bound and frightened Sheriff, together with Hubert and the eight sentries, smelt a rare good meal cooking in the outlaws' secret glade, and wondered if they would be hanged before it was eaten. All had sore heads after the terrific buffet that had been given to each when he was captured, and the Sheriff's head was the sorest of all, for Little John had dealt him his buffet.

Robin Hood himself came to his prisoners while the outlaws' meal was still sending forth its savoury odours, and ordered that the Sheriff should be unbound and set at liberty.

"But make no attempt at escape," he warned, "for as certainly as you try to get out from this glade, just as surely will an arrow find your heart, Sheriff Robert. I will see that your men are fed, and will have you yourself to dine with me to-day."

"That I never will," the Sheriff retorted.

"Starve then," said Robin, "but you shall starve tied up, and with two lusty men to lash you with wands while I and my men eat, if you treat my invitation with such discourtesy. Which will you choose?"

"There is no choice," said the Sheriff sullenly.

Thus, to the joy of all the band, the High Sheriff of Nottingham sat at their board in company with Robin Hood and the rest, but he made a poor meal, though Marian herself saw that he had the best of everything, and Friar Tuck pointed out the virtue of good appetite, while Little John devoured great hunks of venison. When they had finished, Robin

called to the Sheriff to move up along the board and
sit facing him.

"For there is a reckoning for all things, Sheriff," he
said, "even for a meal with the king of Sherwood.
How much shall he pay, Friar Tuck?"

"Seeing that he is a man of substance, let him put
down the reward he hath offered for your head—
fifty marks in gold," said the friar.

"What say you, Little John?"

"Well," said Little John, eyeing the Sheriff, "he is a
lean and ill-favoured beast, over-spare in the flank
and mean in the face, but an he count himself not
worth fifty marks in gold then we must hang him."

"But I have no fifty marks with me," said the
Sheriff.

"We will keep a hostage when you have agreed
the sum," Robin Hood explained. "Do you consent to
ransom yourself?"

"It is better than a hanging," the Sheriff retorted.

"Then swear, on the cross hilt of my sword, that
the sum shall be put under the dead oak by Dark
Mere within three days after you get back to home
and wife in Nottingham."

The Sheriff looked up at the sky and down at the
ground, for it went to his heart to swear to any such
bond. But when he saw that Little John had hold of
a rope, and was knotting a noose in the end, he
swore the oath most hastily.

"Now there is another small matter," said Robin
Hood. "Marian, fetch me an inkhorn and a quill,
dear wife, for our Sheriff can surely write his name,
seeing what his station is."

He took an arrow from the quiver on the ground

beside him, and laid it on the board before the Sheriff as Marian brought the pen and ink. Dipping the pen in the inkhorn, he handed it to Robert de Rainault.

"Now on the shaft of that arrow, Sheriff, write your own name," he bade. "See that you write it fairly and well, too."

Reluctantly the Sheriff complied. Robin inspected the arrow when the writing was finished, and nodded approval.

"It will serve," he said. "Sheriff, you have set out a reward for me, you have threatened to hang me, and you have come into Sherwood to hunt me down as I hunt the deer in this forest. I have been patient with you thus far, and have done you and your men no harm, but now I tell you that as surely as you move against me again, just so surely shall this arrow that bears your name be sent through your evil heart."

The Sheriff stared at the arrow and made no answer.

"You shall go back to Nottingham this night," Robin pursued, "and see that you remember the oath you swore, and that fifty marks in gold lie under the dead oak by Dark Mere in three days' time."

"The gold shall be there," said the Sheriff.

"Else," said Robin, "it will be the worse for a man you hold as worth somewhat to you. For I will keep your man Hubert here, and if the gold be not paid he hangs. Already, I know, he hath killed a man at your bidding, for no crime at all except that the man was a Saxon and held land of you that you wanted back, but even for this I will not punish either him or you, so long as you keep your word."

"I have both sworn and said the gold shall be there," the Sheriff retorted sullenly. "I can do no more."

"Then wait here till nightfall," Robin ordered.

This last order irked the Sheriff very much, for he had hoped to go out in daylight, and so get some hint of the precise spot in which this strong retreat of Robin's band was located. But he had to wait till nightfall, when suddenly Little John seized him as he walked among the huts, and a coarse sack was put over his head, after which his hands and feet were tied.

"We mean no harm, Sheriff," Little John told him, "but it is our leader's order that you travel in this fashion."

They tied him on a mule and led it out from the glade. For hours, it seemed to the Sheriff, the beast plodded on in silence, until, suddenly, the sack was ripped from his head and he saw the stars twinkling above. Somebody gripped the back of his neck, and he opened his mouth to cry out, when a wad of linen was stuffed in it and tied hastily with a kerchief that went round and behind his head. Then, as they lifted him off the mule, he saw a great wall before him, and knew it for the wall of his city of Nottingham.

There just outside the gate, the outlaws laid him down carefully and silently, and there they left him.

CHAPTER II / How They Got Will Scarlett Back

WITHIN the castle yard of Evil Hold was bustle and excitement, for, in addition to the ordinary tasks of the morning, there was the business of putting up a tall gallows for the hanging of Will Scarlett, captured the previous day, and Isambart himself, together with his friend Roger the Cruel, strode about, the two of them in full armour, bestowing an order here and a kick on some unfortunate worker there. Isambart was in high good humour, for nobody but himself had ever been able to lay hands on any man of Robin's band.

The bustle and excitement were at their highest when a tattered old man drove up to the drawbridge, passed the man on sentry duty without being questioned, since both the horse and cart were well known, and passed through the low arch in the great wall that shut in the castle yard and formed the outer defence of the great keep, in which were Isambart's living-rooms, with the dungeons under them. In the entry to the arch, the old man reached back to one of his bundles, jerked the string off the mouth of the sack, and with a push let loose a beehive, which went rolling back toward the guard-house, away from the darkness of the arch.

Taking no notice, the old man, who was Robin Hood disguised, drove on, straight toward the keep. He was within ten yards of its open portal when Isambart spied him.

"Hey, old fool!" Isambart yelled. "Think you that we store our wood in our banqueting hall? Fetch your cart here!"

Staring at him stupidly, the old man fumbled with the string of his second sack. Isambart took a couple of steps toward the cart, but stopped as a tremendous yelling and screaming came from the direction of the guard-house. Then the old man got the string off his sack, gave it a push, and out toppled Robin's second beehive at Isambart's feet, just as Robin pulled down the gauze over his face and neck from under his hat, and made a flying leap that landed him almost in the doorway of the keep.

A great cloud of angry bees rose up all over the castle yard, just as the door of the keep slammed in Isambart's face, and he heard the sound of the great bolts being shot home. Then the horse, stung by half a dozen bees at once, shot forward and scattered a group of Isambart's men who were running toward their master, while first Isambart himself, and then Roger the Cruel, yelled and danced as the bees got under their armour and began to sting. They slapped at the hard metal they wore, and made matters worse, while Isambart's men ran all ways.

Some of them ran out under the arch toward the drawbridge, but there they met a second angry swarm in possession. The men on guard had bolted for the moat, and stood in the shallows with only the tops of their heads showing, except when they bobbed up for breath, to find the bees waiting to take vengeance on them. Isambart and his men ran hither and thither, yelling and shouting, and wherever they ran the bees followed, hot and angry. Since the castle had been built for a stronghold, there was

no way in except that of the great entrance which
Robin Hood had barred from the inside, and no way
out except past the guard-house, so here were Isambart and his men penned in the yard, absolutely at
the mercy of the bees.

Roger the Cruel, rolling on the ground and
squealing as the stings got at him under his armour,
spied a dark storehouse built in the outer walls, and
made for its shelter, yelling and slapping himself all
over, just as a great arrow hummed over the wall
and thudded into the earth at Isambart's feet. Isambart, dancing and slapping with his gauntleted hands,
stared at it.

"Attacked—attacked by Robin Hood's band!" he
shouted. "To me, men, and lower away at the portcullis! Up with the drawbridge!"

But the bees were keeping his men busy, and they
crowded round the dark doorway in which Roger the
Cruel was trying to shelter himself, with a little
cloud of bees buzzing spitefully around the head of
every one of them. Isambart's shout went unheard,
for they were all shouting at once, and Isambart
himself, stopping every now and again to dance and
slap himself, made for the chamber in the wall in
which was the portcullis gear, to lower it and keep
the outlaws out, for now the arrows began to fall
thick and fast, and already three of his men were
wounded by them before they could get to the shelter of the wall.

Inside the great keep Robin darted into a little
room on the right of the doorway, where the only
man on guard lounged carelessly. In ten seconds the
man was lying stunned by a blow from the heavy
cudgel Robin carried in addition to his sword, and

Robin had the bunch of keys which he saw lying on the table. As the uproar began among the bees outside, Robin swung the heavy door which led to the great hall of the keep and the upper apartments, locking it with one of the keys he had taken, and then with another key he unlocked a door at the head of a stairway that led down into the passageway between the dungeons. He locked this door behind him, knowing that he would not return that way.

"Ho, guards!" he shouted, when he came to the foot of the stair, into a gloomy corridor lighted only by one torch at its far end. "Out and help to man the walls—the castle is attacked!"

Three men ran out into the corridor. The first of them was bare from the waist upward, and wore a black mask over his face. Robin knew him for Isambart's head torturer and executioner, and with a run at him brought down his cudgel on the man's head with such force that the rascal never moved again. Another was down before they could realize that they were being attacked, and, as the third drew a dagger, Robin hurled himself on him and brought him down on the stone floor with a crash. Seeing that he, too, was stunned, Robin dragged him and his fellow into one of the dungeons and turned the key on them. Having executed the executioner, he troubled no more about him, but left him lying.

"Scarlett?" he shouted. "Where are you, good Will?" "Scarlett?" he shouted. "Where are you, good Will?"

"Here I be!" came a weak voice from the corridor. Robin went along warily, passing a great chamber through the doorway of which shone a red glow from the fire in which the executioner had been heating his implements of torture, and other doors from which unfortunate victims of Isambart's cruelty called out or moaned as he passed. He called again to make sure of the cell in which Scarlett had been placed, found the right key, and flung the door open.

Will Scareltt staggered out, a bloodstained bandage round his head. "I knew you would not fail me, Robin," he said weakly, "but I doubt if I have strength to win back to the greenwood. They have wounded me sorely."

"Courage, good Will," said Robin, "and a breath of fresh air outside this unwholesome place will work wonders. But I think we have time to unlock a few of these doors as we go. We may win aid from those within, if we could only arm them."

Door after door he unlocked as they went along the corridor to the foot of the stairway, and out crawled a dozen pallid wretches who would have kissed his feet in thankfulness had he let them, while there were four stout fellows who had not been long confined, and one tall man who bowed courteously to Robin and thanked him for his deliverance.

He had now five good men, in addition to those who were so weak from long imprisonment that they were useless, and he set two of them to help Will Scarlett along. He found a low-set door in the wall at the foot of the stairs, and, unlocking it, disclosed the black darkness of a slimy passage.

Just then they heard faintly the sound of great thunderous blows above their heads, and Robin smiled grimly at the noise.

"That is Isambart, past doubt," he said. "He is trying to batter in his own front door, by the sound of it."

And so it was, for since Robin had locked the door of the great inner hall, nobody could get at the bolts of the outer door from its inside to open it, and Isambart's only chance was to batter it down, though he knew it would take a good month of carpenters' and smiths' work to make him another like it, to say nothing of the damage to the masonry.

"We must e'en go this way," said Robin, gazing into the darkness of the passage. "One of you fetch me the torch from the far end of the corridor, and I will lead the way."

When the torch was brought he advanced into the passage. For nearly a quarter of a mile, they judged, they tramped through the dripping, slimy way, until before them daylight showed through the keyhole of an iron door.

"Now let us pray that I have the key of this door," Robin said, and sought among those he had brought. Among them was one that fitted, and he led the way out into a deep arch, beyond which showed the brilliant sunshine of the day.

They found themselves standing at the top of a steep slope, with the castle wall behind them, and before them the depths of the moat. Beyond in the distance, waiting for them, lay a body of Robin's men, among whom Little John stood up and waved to them to announce that they had been seen, after which he sank down again into the grass.

"We must swim for it," Robin said. "Come on, Will, and let me give you a hand across."

The tall man who had thanked him stepped forward. "Good sir," he said, "do you let me take one side of him."

"Willingly," said Robin, "but who may you be that talk like a Norman, and yet lie in prison at a Norman knight's hands?"

"I am a knight, Sir Richard at Lea," said the other.

"Mercy on us!" Robin ejaculated, startled. "But let us get across this water before we talk about it."

He led the way down the bank, helping Scarlett as he went, and Sir Richard gave the wounded man a lift on his other side. They got across and climbed out, followed by the four men who had had strength to arm themselves, and by two other prisoners. The rest, hopeless and hardly sane after years of Isambart's cruelties, dared not trust themselves to swim the moat, and stood by the archway in the wall, staring stupidly.

"Poor wretches," Robin said, looking back at them, "I would that we could have saved them. Let us march quickly."

A little later, a troop of a dozen horsemen clattered out over the drawbridge, rounded the moat, and galloped across the open to cut off the fleeing men. Then from under the rags that disguised him Robin took the silver bugle he had won in the tournament at Nottingham, and blew five blasts on it.

And from the edge of the wood to which Robin and his party advanced there hummed and sang flight after flight of great arrows toward the pursuing horsemen, so that within a minute half their horses were down, and the rest were bolting. Robin blew one short blast, and the arrow showers ceased.

"Man," said Sir Richard at Lea, "are you a magician?"

CHAPTER 12 / News from the East

WHILE Sir Richard wondered, Robin Hood went on toward the forest shades, where, as his men gathered round him and the rescued Will Scarlett, the knight marvelled still more.

"See to our good Will, Little John," Robin bade, "for they have given him a nasty cut over the head, and we must carry him back to our retreat." He turned then to the knight. "And you, sir, though you give me an impossible name, will perhaps come with us for rest and food?"

"Right gladly," the knight answered. "But why do you call the name I gave you impossible?"

"For that Sir Richard at Lea was drowned in the ship that was sunk when he went to join our King Richard fighting in the Holy Land. That is an old tale, and I must be the magician you called me if I rescue a dead man from Isambart's dungeons."

"Isambart's dungeons?" the knight echoed. "But they were the dungeons of Roger whom they call the Cruel. I never saw Isambart de Belame, all the time of my imprisonment."

"This, then, is a mystery," Robin said, puzzled. "Good knight, tell us all your tale as we go back to our camp, and know yourself safe in Sherwood with Robin Hood and his band."

"And who may they be?" the knight asked.

"You mean that you have never heard of Robin

Hood?" Little John asked in amazement. "Where have you been?"

"Jailed from all knowledge these four years past," Sir Richard answered sadly, "so that I know not if my dear daughter be living, nor what hath passed in the outer world."

"Then tell us all the tale," Robin bade.

"The tale begins with my wife's dying," the knight said, "at which I determined to go and fight the Saracen with our great king, for so I might forget my grief awhile. Thus I gave my daughter Marian into charge of Abbot Hugo of St. Mary's, and agreed with him that she should be sent to Kirklees. Then, having but little ready money, I borrowed five hundred marks from the Abbot for my gear and the hire of a ship for me and my men, agreeing to pay him fifty marks a year for the use of the money when I should return, and pledging my chief manor as proof that I would pay him. So he holds the deeds of the manor to this day."

"Even so," said Robin, "and I might have guessed the hand of Abbot Hugo in this dark tale. But tell us the rest."

"Having made all ready, and bidden farewell to my sweet daughter, I took my men to Hull, and there we set sail in a ship bound for Bordeaux, where I had been told I should find others assembling on my errand. But a storm came out of the east when we had been but three hours at sea, and we drove on to the Lincolnshire coast. Whether any other man was saved out of the wreck I do not know, but I was lifted ashore on the end of a broken spar to which I clung, sore wounded with a great cut in the head, and near on senseless. To the men who found me I had strength to bid that they take me to St. Mary's Abbey, and after that I remember no more, for a fever came of the great wound I had got."

"So you do not know if you came to St. Mary's Abbey?" Robin asked.

"I have memory, like a dream, of Abbot Hugo and Roger the Cruel talking together," Sir Richard answered, "and after that a great darkness as the fever came again. I wakened in the dungeons from which you released me."

"And for how long does the bond hold under which you borrowed the marks from the Abbot?" Robin asked.

"Four years," the knight answered. "Unless it be paid by Michaelmas Day of this year, then my best manor lands are forfeit to Abbot Hugo."

"Even so," and Robin nodded, "and all the plot is clear. He would keep you jailed, since even he dare not have you killed, for the full four years, and then the manor would fall to him. Also he would have you think it was Roger the Cruel who held you prisoner, and not Isambart de Belame, for he would have married your daughter Marian to Belame. Now there are yet seven weeks to Michaelmas Day, good Sir Richard."

"And the bond is for seven hundred marks!" said Sir Richard, "while if it were but seven I could not pay it."

"Rest content on that, Sir Richard, and I will lend you the money," Robin said. "It is but a small sum to us."

"Why," said Sir Richard, "only a king could call it a small sum, and who are you that talk so?"

"King in Sherwood, and some small relative to you

by marriage," Robin answered with a laugh. "You shall see."

For now, marching through the forest shades, they drew near the outlaws' retreat, and began to descend the path in the side of the cliff that led to their hidden glade. Sir Richard shook his head in a puzzled way as he saw the huts in the valley.

"Nay," he said, "for I know all my dead wife's people, and there was none like you among them."

But now Marian came running toward the path, for, like the good wife she was, she had waited in fear till she could learn how Robin had fared over his daring venture into Evil Hold. With no eyes for any other, she flung herself into Robin's arms.

"I could do naught but sit and pray for you," she said, "and all the time I feared for you, in that den of evil men."

Robin kissed her and held her back from him. "We are all safe, and Scarlett back with us with a wound for you to heal, Marian," he said. "But look about you, and see if you know any of those we bring with us."

Then, with a great cry of joy, she was in Sir Richard's arms, folded close to his heart. "Oh, we all thought you dead!" she cried happily. "Robin, this is too wonderful."

The knight looked at his rescuer over Marian's head. "Sir," he said, "I know not who you are or why you are here, but in one day you have restored to me my freedom and my daughter, though why she should first come to your arms——"

"Plague on it!" said Robin with a laugh, "may not a man's own wife kiss him when he comes back?"

"I could wish her no better husband, from the

little I know of him," Sir Richard said. "Yet there is a smack of outlawry about this wild place, and if that is not venison I smell cooking, I know not the scent of deer meat. Yet it is no affair of mine."

"Good Sir Richard," said Robin, "some of that same venison shall speedily be your affair, and we will make this a feast day in honour of your release and that of my stout Will Scarlett, whose good wife gave me the two hives of bees that made such a rout of Isambart and his men in the castle yard, while I came looking for you. Marian, set Friar Tuck to work dressing the meat from our larder, and when you tell him who is our guest I warrant he will excel himself as a cook."

Right merrily did they feast on venison and the meat of the wild boar, and fat geese and pheasants, with good white bread such as was seldom seen in those days except at the tables of the nobles, while Sir Richard looked at his daughter's happy face as if he could never take his eyes from her.

CHAPTER 13 / The Black Knight Appears

AND now Fortune, which so far had befriended Robin, deserted him, for while he was absent on a distant foray Isambart de Belame burned out the glade, and carried off Marian to Evil Hold, with five of Robin's good men.

Dusk was falling when Robin and his party dismounted on the edge of the woods, and looked out on Evil Hold.

"Look, good Robin," said Little John, with a sob in his voice, and pointed toward the great castle on its height. "In one way we are too late to aid, for we shall speak with those five no more."

Above the outer wall of the castle reared a skeleton framework, and on it swung five black figures, still and ominous. A long time Robin looked at his dead men in silence, and then he drew his sword and put the cross of its hilt against his lips.

"By our Lady the Virgin," he said slowly, "I will not rest from war against this evil man until he is lifeless as are they. By dawn I will have a plan to make an end of Isambart."

"But who comes here?" Little John asked.

From the direction of the castle a strange knight came toward them, riding a great black horse, and armed all in black, with visor down. It was strange that he neither reined in nor showed any sign of alarm at sight of more than a score of armed men on the track, for in those troubled times such a lone rider might expect attack. But he came on like a tower of black iron, and they saw a great battle-axe hanging by his saddle bow.

"A bold man," said Robin, admiringly. "Knight," he called, "what do you ride at on these forest ways?"

The Black Knight reined in, and when he spoke his voice sounded hollow from between the bars of his visor.

"I do as I will, to whom I will," he answered, "but for this present I seek shelter for my horse and myself in the forest."

"Yet there is a strong castle behind you would give shelter," Robin pointed out, "if you are on Count John's affairs."

"Count John's affairs are near my own," said the knight.

"Then in that castle is a man of his, and we will have pleasure in killing you with him when we set about the castle," Robin said. "Get you gone, for we, being more than a score, would not set about one man."

"There is a mystery here," the knight said thoughtfully, "for you are not armed as Normans arm, nor as the Saxons. And why do you propose to attack yonder castle?"

"For many reasons," Robin answered, "which you, being John's man, may not hear. Get gone, to the castle or elsewhere."

"Though John's affairs are very near mine, I am not John's man," the knight answered, "and if there be cause for the pulling down of that castle I might help. But is there cause?"

"Right good cause," Robin answered. "If you

should care to eat with us, I can tell you some of the cause, good knight, and you may see whether it is worth while to swing that great axe of yours beside us—or against us. For if you are for that castle's owner, it will give me great pleasure to kill you."

The Black Knight dismounted from his horse, a great, strong figure of a man. "I will eat with you," he said, "and we may discuss this matter while we eat. To my thought, these strong castles are too plentiful about the country, but whether this one should be attacked or no is matter for grave thought. You shall state your reasons."

So, when they had all tended their horses, and settled round a fire deeply set in the forest shade, so that Isambart's sentries could not see the flame, Robin told the tale of how Sir Richard at Lea had been imprisoned in Evil Hold for nearly four years, so that Abbot Hugo might have his manor and Isambart might have his daughter and the rest of his lands. The Black Knight, who had raised his visor to eat, but kept his helmet on so that they could see little of his face, listened to the story.

"Right well I know that Sir Richard," he said, "for I was present when he was knighted by King Henry. But where do you who tell this tale come into it? What have Sir Richard's woes to do with you?"

"Sir Richard's daughter is my wife," Robin answered.

"Yet even then, since you have the maid as your wife, and this Sir Isambart have not harmed you, it is not your quarrel," said the knight.

Robin pointed through the trees in the direction of the castle. "She lies prisoner in that hold, captured in my absence, when this Sir Isambart burned my home and took my men to hang them from his castle wall," he said. "Knight, by your talk you are Norman, but so is my wife's father, for there are some good Normans, and I would that the best of them all, our King Richard, were back to right some of these wrongs in England. If you choose to help us, then we are glad of you."

"Of a surety I will help you," the Black Knight promised, "for of this burning of homes and carrying off of women—aye, and hanging of men too!—there is too much, and it is time these robber barons were taught their lesson. But how will you, with not more than a score men, go up against such a castle as that?"

"Aye, how, good Robin?" asked Little John. "Shall we sit under the wall and scratch a hole in it with our finger nails?"

"What name was that he called you?" the knight asked.

"My own name—Robin Hood. But remember, good knight, you have promised us your aid!"

The knight laughed softly to himself, and for a few moments sat in thought. "Aye, I have promised," he said at last. "Yet, Robin Hood, will you scratch a hole in the wall of the castle and crawl through, as your man here asked just now? For it is no small thing to attack such a place."

"I have thirty more men to come," Robin said shortly, "and when it is time I will scratch you such a hole in the wall of this castle as shall leave it toppling, if a dozen of the best of you come with me."

"You have a plan then?" the knight asked.

"I have more, a key by which to enter the very

keep itself. For when I had rescued Sir Richard along with my own man from their dungeons, I kept the key of the postern at back of the castle, and now wait only for the rest of my men to come up before attacking from the inside, and opening the gate to the main party of my men."

"A bold game to play, outlaw," he said, "but ever the bold game wins. When your men come up, I will either come with you by the postern, or lead the main attack for you, as you will."

Robin looked at the knight's mighty frame. "Then lead me the main attack," he said, "for craft will mainly serve inside, but such strength as yours will be needed in the main attack."

The knight sat looking into the embers of their fire, as if deep in thought. Then he stood up.

"I will go and sleep by my horse," he said, "but you have given me much on which to think, Robin Hood. Some day, perhaps, you may know my name, but before that I will help you in this business of the castle over on the hill there, for that is a foul tyrant who hath no place within the law or out of it."

CHAPTER 14 / The End of Evil Hold

WREATHS of autumn mist shrouded the forest ways next day when Friar Tuck tramped in with the rest of Robin Hood's men and asked what plans Robin had made for the attack on Evil Hold. The Black Knight—for they knew him by no other name— stood by and listened while Robin told his men how Isambart had hanged the five he had captured, and many a promise of vengeance was made as they heard.

"Now, for the sake of Marian, we must lose no time," Robin said. "This knight hath promised me that he will lead the attack on the main gateway of the castle, while I, who know of a way in, will take a score of you who can swim, and attack from the inside while Isambart and his men are busy defending the drawbridge."

"But," said the knight, at whom all looked as he stood among them with his visor down, "there must be some signal, so that neither your men nor those I lead attack too soon, for else this Isambart will dispose of one party first and then turn on the other."

"Signal enough," Robin answered, "for I with these men swim the moat at the back of the castle, and when you see us up against the wall itself, then do you attack in front. They will muster to resist you, and leave me to do what I will in the keep. And I want Dickon of Hartshead, who helped in the building of the place, to come with me and show me the ways of it, since Marian is prisoned there."

He took Little John, and Dickon, and eighteen more, armed only with swords, since he reckoned on getting at Isambart's armoury, once they were inside, and knew that if they took bows the strings would only get wetted and useless in crossing the moat. They could not have had a better day, for mists lay over all the countryside, and, moving as only foresters can, they were able to make their way to the very edge of the moat unseen. As it was, they came up toward the back of the castle, where little or no watch was kept, and there waited awhile, for the mists were deepening to fog, and Robin hoped, if it thickened a little more, to swim the moat unseen by the men who walked the walls.

Unseen he crossed, a little after noon, and helped man after man up the inner bank until all were across. Then they crawled warily up the steep slope and gained the shelter of the archway which hid the iron door leading into Isambart's secret passage, and then the chain of watchers whom the knight and Friar Tuck had posted passed back word that it was time to begin the main attack, at which the larger party of the outlaws, led by the Black Knight, moved out from the forest toward the gate.

The key of the iron door squealed in its rusty lock as Robin turned it, and as he thrust the door open he heard a shout from the battlements, at which he feared lest he had been seen in the archway. But it was the cry passed on from Isambart that the main gate was about to be attacked, and after it a trumpet blew for the assembly of the castle garrison. One by one Robin and his men filed into the secret way, and in single file marched down it, in pitch darkness, for after their crossing of the moat they had no means of making a light.

Cut off from all hearing of what was passing above them, they reached the door that gave on to the corridor of dungeons and Isambart's torture chamber, and here Robin, who had kept only the one key, called forward Little John to come up beside him.

" 'Tis but a flimsy door of wood, John," he whispered, "and I have no key to it. But it opens outward, and your great shoulder may serve with my help to make us a way."

He put his own shoulder against the door, and felt it give slightly. For a moment they listened, but there was no sound in the corridor beyond, and then Little John put his mighty bulk against the door with Robin. At a tremendous heave by them both the woodwork about the lock splintered and gave way, and they half fell into the dim light of the dungeon corridor. A moaning came from one of the cells, but no other sound.

"Dickon," Robin bade one of his followers, "before our work here is finished, do you get the keys of these cells and let loose any poor wretches you find within. But now we have another door to force at the top of these stairs, before we win out to the entrance of the keep itself."

He went forward into the torture chamber, which was unlighted now, and there found two great hammers used for riveting fetters on Isambart's prisoners. One he took for himself, and the other for Little John, and led the way up the stair.

"Stand back, Robin," Little John bade, "and give me that heavier hammer, for there is room for but one to swing a blow, here."

He felt about the door till he had found its lock, while one of the band passed up the torch which burned at the far end of the dungeon corridor. Little John spat on his hands, took a grip of the great hammer, and whirled it above his head, bringing it down with a crash on the lock of the door. They saw a crack of light show beyond, and gripped their swords as the hammer swung again, and with a second crashing blow burst them a way out to the entrance of the keep.

Four men, whom Isambart had left to guard his prisoners when he went to the defence of the drawbridge, started forward, but Little John's hammer took one in the chest and sent him flying against another, so that two were down with the one blow. Robin accounted for a third, and the fourth bolted with a yell for Isambart's great hall, but never reached it, for the whole score of Robin's men were close behind him, hot and eager. They surged into the hall, and paused, for at the far side, bound in a chair, sat Marian all alone, with a great parchment spread on the table before her, and an inkhorn and quill beside it.

"Robin!" she cried. "Robin—he would have made me sign away my lands to him, but I would not."

"Time for that afterward, dear wife," Robin answered, stooping to kiss her as he drew his sword to cut her bonds. "Now, any two of you but Dickon or Little John, take her out by the secret passage, and across the moat to safety. Here is no place for women, if we would win the castle."

He stayed but for a word more with her, but, as two volunteered to escort her out to the safety of the forest, followed Dickon of Hartshead to Isambart's armoury. A dozen of his men went out to the shattered door of the keep, which Isambart himself had had to batter down after Robin had locked him out of his own castle, and which had not yet been repaired. While Robin and Dickon were busy getting bows, these dozen had to stand the attack of Roger the Cruel and half a score men-at-arms who had seen that all was not well inside the castle. Little John crashed Roger to earth as a great arrow sang by his ear and pinned another man so that he fell, and Robin shouted joyfully. "Bows, men—bows for all! Stand aside and let us at them!"

The dozen fell back against the walls, and a hail of arrows finished off the men Roger had fetched. Now they could hear the roaring attack that went on by the drawbridge, led by the Black Knight, and Robin served out a bow and full quiver from Isambart's armoury to each man.

"Out and at them," he bade, "while they meet the attack from outside."

The Black Knight had led his party on with a rush, and they came at the drawbridge out of the mist while Little John was battering a way through the door at the top of the dungeon stair; Friar Tuck, puffing as he ran, bore the biggest ladder he could find, to help in crossing the moat if they were too late to win the drawbridge, and two others also carried ladders they had taken from a farm nearby. The Black Knight, leading the whole of them in spite of his armour, was still a score yards from the end of the drawbridge when the alarm sounded within the castle wall and the end of the bridge swung into the air, for their advance had been seen by the sentry on the wall.

"Into the moat with the ladders!" the Black Knight commanded. "They will save us from sinking in our armour." For Robin's men were heavily armed, while the knight himself was in complete mail from head to foot. And never had they seen a man so active; he was like a cat on his feet, in spite of the weight of metal he carried.

Splash went the ladders at his word, and he leaped into the water, grasping one and pushing it across as he swam. Crossbow bolts rattled on him, but they were no more than flies buzzing, for all the notice he took of them. Friar Tuck, who plunged in beside him, grabbed the end of the ladder just in time as the water closed over his head, and came up blowing like a whale.

"I had sooner drink wine," he remarked. "This moat hath an unpleasant flavour, like its owner."

The other ladders pitched in, and by the aid of all three a dozen men got safely across while the rest of the band made the crossbowmen keep away from the slits in the wall, for arrows hailed through with deadly accuracy, and though Isambart cursed and raved at his men he could not get them to face the shafts from the long bows. The Black Knight and Friar Tuck hauled up their ladder and stood under the shelter of the wall, and Isambart, spying them, yelled to his men to tumble stones down on them. But as surely as a man tried to roll a stone over, an arrow found him, for the party on the other side of the moat had eyes keen enough to pierce the mist.

They could not have chosen a better time, had

they known it, for Isambart had lost heavily in his attack on the forest stronghold when he carried off Marian, and he had twenty men out on a raiding party as well, while Robin and his men inside had already accounted for Roger the Cruel and more than a dozen of the garrison. There were not sixty men in all to aid Isambart in holding the gate, though the proper strength of the castle was rated at not less than a hundred, and of these sixty a dozen were already dead or wounded by the arrows that flew with such deadly accuracy from Robin's men.

Inside, Robin could see across the yard the open recess in the wall, above the entrance arch, in which was the gear for raising and lowering the drawbridge and portcullis. He could see, too, how Isambart tried to get his men up for the defence and knew that all was not well with them.

"Now," he said, "if some dozen of you here keep us a clear way to the drawbridge gear with your bows, the rest of us may charge across and lower the bridge for our fellows outside, and mayhap get the portcullis up as well. To me, Little John, and four more—the rest to your bows, and spare not the arrows."

They went at it with a run, and were almost at the gatehouse before Isambart spied them. He roared to his men to guard the stair, but the humming arrows made it a place of death, and Robin and Little John, who still carried his great hammer, were at the top before a man could come at them. By the time Isambart's men thought to counter the attack with crossbows, Robin's party were safe in the open recess, and still the flying arrows kept back those who would attack. Isambart himself tried it, but so many arrows

rattled on his mail that he was literally driven back
by their weight, and could not come at the recess,
for all the defences of the castle were constructed to
stand attack from outside, not within, and against
men shooting from the door of their own keep the
defenders were helpless.

Now with a dozen great blows of his hammer
Little John smashed the ratchet that held up the
bridge, and it crashed down with such force that it
broke in half, yet left enough for Robin's men outside to cross by it, wet-footed. Then Little John and
Robin each took one of the windlasses of the portcullis, and slowly it began to rise as the outlaws poured
across the bridge.

First through the rising portcullis was Friar Tuck
his robe tucked up in his girdle, and a sword in his
hand—but there was nobody to strike, for all Isambart's men that were left on their feet fled toward
the keep. Isambart himself, mailed and with his visor down, stood his ground, and Friar Tuck would
have made at him, but the Black Knight held him
back.

"My baron—my quarrel," he said, words which
the friar could not then understand. But the knight's
hand on his shoulder wrenched him back as Robin
came running down from the windlass recess, eager
to engage with the man who had carried off his wife

"Back!" the Black Knight ordered, in a tone there
was no disputing. "This man is mine—I will engage
him."

At the order all men stood still to watch, except
those who fought with Isambart's followers in the
entrance of the keep. They saw how the Black

Knight came up to Isambart, apparently careless, with his battle-axe swinging lightly in his hand, though it was of a weight that few men would have cared to swing. When Isambart thrust at him with his long sword he was not in the way of the thrust, for he moved like lightning, yet always with apparent carelessness. Three times Isambart thrust, and three times the thrust went wide, before the battle-axe flashed and fell once only, and Isambart crashed to earth to move no more.

Then a cry from the gateway of the keep warned Robin that his men there were hard beset, and he ran to their aid. By the time that business was finished, there was no more resistance left, but Evil Hold was at the mercy of him and his men. And now at a thought he swung round suddenly, looking out into the castle yard.

"The Black Knight—where is he?" he shouted.

"Legging it, Robin," Friar Tuck answered. "For he went out through the arch and over the bridge, and by this time, if he keep the pace at which he started, he hath reached his horse and gone, without a word of farewell to any of us."

"We might have known it," Robin said regretfully. "If any man of you see that knight again, on your knees to him and beg mercy. Only one man in the world swings a battle-axe in such fashion, and only one man is so like a cat on his feet. That was our King Richard, and we were all blind not to know him."

"King or cat, there he goes," Little John said, and pointed.

And, through the opening under the raised portcullis, they could see the Black Knight's horse trotting away toward the forest. Robin shook his head regretfully.

"Still, he helped us, and had he not approved us he would not have done that," he said. "Now I know why he kept his helmet and refused to tell his name. They say he has left not a castle standing in Lincolnshire, and he used his strength to help us make an end of this Evil Hold."

"It still stands," Little John reminded him.

"But not for long," Robin said, "for as we have made an end of the master, so will we make an end of his hold, lest some other evil baron come to oppress the people round."

He bade them take barrels of pitch, of which there was plenty, and place one in each room of the great keep, together with all the firewood they could find. When all women in hiding had been sought out and sent from the castle, and the prisoners had been released, they fired the place, and from every window and arrow slit the black smoke streamed out on the misty air, to be presently shot with tongues of flame. They shattered the windlasses of the portcullis, so that it could be raised no more, and the drawbridge was already a broken thing. A party of them dug at the outer bank of the moat where it was lowest, and all the water went flowing out across the plain, so that there was no outer defence left for the wall, and in later days men came and took away the stones for building their homes.

But the great keep flamed up, a pillar of fire visible for miles round, and the poor people whom Isambart had oppressed and taxed came and blessed Robin Hood and his men for the work they had done in freeing them from a wicked tyrant. Far into the night the castle blazed like a torch, and in the end went crashing down to a mere heap of cracked stones, over which brambles grew in later days, and foxes made their earths among them.

But Roger the Cruel, recovering in time from the great blow that had laid him low, crept away while the Black Knight and Isambart fought together, and made his way down the dungeon stair, out by the secret passage, and across the moat. Thus he escaped his just doom, and out of that came bitter trouble in a later day.

CHAPTER 15 / How Sir Richard
Paid His Debt

ABBOT HUGO, rejoicing when Isambart de Belame captured and burnt the outlaw stronghold in the forest was sore dismayed when he learned that Robin Hood and his men had taken and burnt Isambart's castle, and, by all accounts, made an end of Isambart himself. He got the news from Roger the Cruel, who, now a ruined man, stole away to St. Mary's Abbey with the tidings, and pointed to the great flame in the sky where Evil Hold burned.

But neither from Roger nor anyone else could the Abbot get news of Sir Richard at Lea. Isambart had kept the knight's escape a secret from Hugo, who for his part hoped most devoutly that Sir Richard had been forgotten in the dugeons and burnt to death when the castle was destroyed. In any case, he counted, Sir Richard could never raise the seven hundred marks he was due to pay at Michaelmas, then kept as a great feast; the manor of Lea would fall to the Abbey on that day, Abbot Hugo reckoned, and even if Sir Richard did appear alive he could put out some tale to clear himself.

He took counsel again with his brother, the Sheriff of Nottingham, with regard to exterminating these dangerous outlaws, but Robert the Sheriff had had enough of hunting them for the time. So Hugo went back to his Abbey in great fear, and prepared to hold his Michaelmas audience in the great hall of the Abbey, where the freemen who held lands of him must

110

come to pay their rents and other dues. The King's Justiciary, then making a tour of the county to see that the laws were kept, was his guest at the Abbey just then, and he sat with Hugo to see the rents paid.

By an hour after noon all was done, and Hugo folded his hands complacently.

"All paid," he said, "and now there is that little matter of the bond Sir Richard at Lea gave to me, which falls due to-day. You, Justiciary, were witness to the bond, by which I now claim the manor of Lea, since Sir Richard hath not appeared to pay."

"Softly, friend," said the Justiciary, "for the day is not over yet, and he may appear before you and pay before night."

Hugo shook his head. "If he had meant to pay, he would have been here before now," he said. "Here is the bond." And he laid the parchment out on the table before them.

The Justiciary studied it. "A right good bargain," he said. "For seven hundred marks you get this great manor and all its farms, worth near on two thousand marks, in all. Abbot, as witness to the bond, am I not entitled to something?"

Hugo poked him in the ribs and chuckled. "Justiciary, there is a bag of a hundred marks lying by, for when I claim the manor. Good payment for your service, eh?"

"If it were known that the King's Justiciary took bribes," the Justiciary replied, "I might lose my head."

"None need know," the Abbot told him. "After we have dined together, I can hand you the bag, and nobody will be the wiser. The King is in Lincolnshire, not in Nottingham or near it. But"—his face

paled and he clutched at the arm of his chair—
"surely that is not Sir Richard?"

But it was Sir Richard at Lea, who entered the
great hall and came forward till he stood before the
Abbot and the Justiciary. With him came a palmer
with the scallop shells on his robe that showed he
had been to the Holy Land, and a great, deep cowl
over his face, so that little more than his eyes
showed. Abbot Hugo gave him only one glance.

"Greeting, Hugo," said Sir Richard. "I have come
about the matter of the bond of mine you hold, for
seven hundred marks, for which my manor of Lea is
in pawn to you."

Hugo recovered his composure with an effort.
"You are late, Sir Richard," he answered, "for by the
letter of the law the bond is due at noon of this day.
Now, I conclude, you have come to pay it."

"Good Hugo," Sir Richard said pleadingly, "could
you not give me a few more days to raise the money?
I have but just escaped from prison, and have had
great misfortunes."

"Not a day can I give you, Sir Richard," the Abbot
answered sternly, recovering his spirits now that he
reckoned on the manor as his own. "We are but poor
churchmen, and I cannot afford it. Your manor must
be forfeit if the money is not paid."

"But it was for the sacred cause of our King's crusade that I borrowed it, and not for my own pleas-
ures," Sir Richard pleaded. "Give me a few days
more, to see if I have any friends."

"Such talk is useless," Hugo retorted. "This day,
not having been paid the money, I claim the manor."

Sir Richard turned to the Justiciary. "Sir," he said,

"can you not plead with him for me? You see my state, that of a knight but just released from prison. Surely he might befriend me so far, rather than take all my lands."

The Justiciary shook his head. "The letter of the law is on his side, Sir Richard," he said, "and I fear I can do nothing." For he thought of the hundred marks the Abbot had promised him, and did not want any delay in seizing the manor, lest he should lose his bribe after all.

"And why bring that tall villain with you?" the Abbot asked scornfully, pointing to the palmer. "We need not witnesses to prove that the money is due to-day, for here is the bond."

"I have not disputed that it is due," Sir Richard answered meekly. "I have but come to beg of you a little charity."

"Charity!" the Abbot snorted contemptuously. "I have the law, and I will hold the manor since you do not pay. Now away with you, knight, for the King's Justiciary here is witness that the money is not paid."

"Not so," Sir Richard answered, with a sudden change of manner. "He shall be witness that it *is* paid!" From under his cloak he took two heavy bags and put them down on the table before the astonished Abbot. "Now that I have found out what the charity of Abbot Hugo is worth, I will take back my bond, for there are your seven hundred marks." And he reached out toward the parchment on the table.

"Not so fast!" Hugo cried. "Let the money be counted, for if it be one mark short, then the bond holds good."

"What of my fee, the hundred marks, Sir Abbot?" the Justiciary broke in, fearing lest he should get nothing.

"Fee?" Hugo echoed. "No, but now I lose the manor—I cannot afford to lose a hundred marks as well."

The clerk stretched out his hand to take the bags and count the money, and the palmer stepped forward and laid a hand on the parchment bond.

"How now, rogue?" the Abbot asked. "That parchment is no concern of yours. Why are you here at all?"

"All this is my concern," the palmer answered, and took up the parchment, scanning it. "Because this good knight needed money to go out to the crusade, Holy Church charged him two hundred marks for the use of five hundred, and the King's Justiciary looked for a bribe of a hundred marks for witnessing the deed."

"What is that to you, you cloaked and cowled scoundrel?" the Abbot asked fiercely. "Here, you men, drub me this thieving palmer out from our hall, and take that parchment from him."

But as the men-at-arms, who waited in the hall under Guy of Gisborne the steward, came forward to obey, the palmer threw back his cowl, and his robe, opening, showed him in full armour under it. And at the sight of his face Guy of Gisborne shrank back, while both the Abbot and the Justiciary rose to their feet, pale as death.

"Hound!" said King Richard. "Who made you Abbot of St. Mary's?"

"Yourself, dread sire," the Abbot moaned. "O, mea culpa—mea maxima culpa, Lord King."

The Justiciary came round the table and knelt at the King's feet, but Richard kicked him away.

"I set you to go about our realm and see that justice was done," he said, "and I find you taking a bribe like any traitor, to break the spirit of the law in keeping its letter. I myself convict you, and deprive you of all office from this day. Your goods and place shall be taken from you—you shall be stripped and sent begging of the people you have wronged—see that it is done, Sir Richard."

Sir Richard bowed, while the Abbot knelt beside his chair.

"As for you, Hugo de Rainault," the King said, "there is a heavy count against you. In a week I set sail for my dominions in France to put all things in order, but be sure that I will return to inquire into this matter of my knight's imprisonment. Your hand in it may yet be proved, and if witnesses can be found to prove it, Holy Church shall not save you, abbot though you be."

"Mercy, sire—mercy!" the Abbot moaned.

"Had you mercy on Sir Richard when he asked for a few days of grace in which to pay your bond? I tell you, de Rainault, when I return from France you shall be brought to trial, and if any other count be added to your oppressions while I am away, for that too you shall be tried."

"Lord King, do I keep my Abbey?" Hugo ventured.

"You hold it for this present," Richard answered sternly, "but on sufferance till our return from France. See that you deal justly and with mercy to all men."

He turned on his heel and stalked out, heedless of

the kneeling figures of Guy of Gisborne and his men. Out in the open, he turned to Sir Richard at Lea.

"Good Sir Richard," he said, "I have had one encounter with this outlaw, Robin Hood, and would fain see him again?"

"Sire," Sir Richard answered, "if he should dream that King Richard sought him, both he and his men would vanish. It must be in disguise, if you go to seek him."

"In disguise let it be, and swiftly, for in a week I must be on my way to London, to set sail for France."

The knight pondered awhile. "Sire," he said at last, "now that you have made Abbot Hugo fear for his place, he will certainly move his valuables out to put them in charge of his brother Robert, the Sheriff of Nottingham, so that he may have something to fall back on when he is thrust out from the Abbey. Just as certainly Robin Hood will have heard that you have faced the Abbot in his hall and accused him, and I warrant that same Robin Hood will know to an hour when the Abbot sets out from St. Mary's to go to his brother. So if you could join the Abbot's party, you might fall in with Robin Hood."

"I will think it over it, good Sir Richard," the King promised. "Now get you to your manor, which you have saved from Abbot Hugo's grasping hands, while I go my own way."

For Prince John was then at Nottingham, and the King wanted a reckoning with his brother.

CHAPTER 16 / The Game of Buffets

WITHIN a week of their return from the burning of
Evil Hold, Robin Hood and his men had repaired the
damage wrought by Isambart in their secret glade,
for the baron's men had overlooked the two caves in
which most of the outlaws' stores were kept, and had
done little beyond burning the huts in the glade,
since they were in a hurry to carry off Marian before
Robin and the greater part of his men could fall on
them. All were eager to prepare for a winter of comfort in the forest depths when, as Sir Richard at Lea
had foretold, Robin got news that the Abbot of St.
Mary's intended to visit his brother at Nottingham.

"And he will surely take at least a part of his hoard
with him," Robin commented, "for since his place as
Abbot is in danger, he will try to lay up a store
against the time when King Richard comes back to
bring him to trial. I would that I had been in the hall
to see our King beard the Abbot and tell him the
truth about himself."

On a clear autumn day, when the brown leaves
fluttered down in the forest, Hugo went his way
toward Nottingham with three friars in attendance,
and Guy of Gisborne with all the men-at-arms the
Abbey could furnish to guard them. Guy with ten
men led the way, and then came the Abbot riding,
with six men leading heavily-laden baggage mules
and the three friars on foot, and behind these, as
rearguard, were another ten men-at-arms. A mer-

chant begged the protection of their escort, and the
Abbot graciously allowed him to join the party as
they entered the forest itself.

They had just crossed an open glen when Robin's
men fell on them, so suddenly that the whole
struggle was over almost as soon as it began. Guy of
Gisborne said that his horse bolted with him, but
whether his spurs helped it was never known,
though he and his ten men were outnumbered three
to one, while the rearguard, seeing men swarming
between them and the Abbot in front, took to their
heels without a blow, so great was their fear of the
outlaws. So there were left the Abbot with his friars
and the mules, and the merchant, who, having no
goods with him, seemed very little disturbed, but
pulled his hat down over his brows and waited on
events.

"Greeting, Hugo," said Robin Hood. "Get down
from that tall horse, and let us have a word together."

Trembling with helpless rage, the Abbot dismounted, and stood with his three monks, while
Robin's men took away those who had led the mules,
and investigated the contents of the packs.

"But a week ago, on Michaelmas Day," said Robin,
"I lent seven hundred good gold marks to St. Mary's
Abbey. It looks as if you have had the goodness to
repay it already, by the packs on these mules."

"I know nothing of that," Hugo interrupted.

"Patience—you will in good time, for the score
against you is a long one," Robin answered. "After
that matter, there is the imprisonment of Sir Richard
at Lea in Evil Hold, for which payment must be
made."

"I had no hand in that!" Hugo cried.

"Friar Tuck, prod that clerk and make him talk," Robin ordered, "for he was witness when Isambart and Roger the Cruel——"

"Nay," the Abbot yelled, "let him keep quiet, and I will confess that too. I shared the guilt of Sir Richard's imprisonment with Isambart."

The merchant, leaning against a tree with two men keeping guard over him, smiled and nodded to himself.

"We will say for that another seven hundred marks, Abbot," Robin suggested, "and so you get off cheaply."

"I am a ruined man!" the Abbot moaned.

"There is also the matter of certain good men I lost when I went to rescue Sir Richard's daughter Marian and burn Evil Hold," Robin pursued calmly. "It is, I know, the custom of such as you to leave the wives and children of such men to starve if the men are killed, but I have another mind about it. A hundred gold marks, to divide among the widows and fatherless children, Abbot, is a small price to pay."

"Robbery and outrage!" the Abbot wailed again.

"The custom of fat abbots is ever robbery and outrage," Robin retorted sternly, "but their sins come back on them at times. Little John, let us look at what the mules carry."

Robin's men, directed by Little John, had been busy stripping the packs off the mules and laying out their contents, which were mainly bags of gold and silver coin, a service of massive silver plate, a bundle of parchment deeds, and some bales of robes and rich cloth which the Abbot had thought he would take to Nottingham to entrust to his brother's care.

"Good store for a ruined man," Robin commented. "Set us aside fifteen hundred marks in payment of the Abbot's just debts, and choose us out the best bale of stuffs for the queen of Sherwood to clothe herself for the winter, Little John, and his holiness shall dance for the rest."

While they counted the money, and the merchant watched them silently, Robin turned to the Abbot again.

"Now, Hugo, our Friar Tuck shall carol us a lively song, and you shall edify us by dancing to it on the turf. Strike up, friar, and let us see the holy man trip a measure."

"But I have rheumatism!" the Abbot protested. "I cannot dance—I am no dancer. Oh, my wealth, my sins! This is an outrage against Holy Church! It is impossible."

"Take an arrow apiece and prick him in the calf, Much and Scarlett," Robin bade, as Friar Tuck began to bellow out a melody. "We will give him a cure for his rheumatism."

At the first touch of the arrow point through his robe the abbot leaped in the air with a squeal, and presently he had gathered up his robe to clear his fat legs, and was hopping and skipping like a mad rabbit. By the time Friar Tuck left off singing, the Abbot was panting for want of breath, and most of Robin's men were helpless with laughter.

"A right good measure, Abbot," Robin said gravely, "and a sure cure for the rheumatism. Now take your clerk, and your monks and mules, and get on your way, but write no more parchments for thieving barons, nor imprison good knights, or it will go far more hardly when I catch you again. If it were not that our good King Richard will bring you to trial in his own time, and I trust hang you for your oppressions, I had not let you go, but I leave you to the justice that is within the law."

The outlaw band watched while the Abbot's men repacked his goods on the mules, and, a sorry and crestfallen gathering, set off on their way.

Little John called out to his chief.

"Ho, Robin, here is a tall merchant still wanting our attention. Do we let him follow the Abbot down to Nottingham?"

"Not so," said Robin. "How much money hath he?"

"Forty marks," Little John answered, "if the count tally with his statement when we asked him."

"Search him and see," Robin bade.

So they stripped back the merchant's long robe, and took off the bag at his waist to count its contents.

"He tells truth," Little John reported, while the merchant stood, with folded arms, "but he hath a fine suit of armour."

"That is his own affair," Robin said. "Being a truthful man we will fine him twenty marks for being in the company of a lying thief like Abbot Hugo, and let him go."

"Now by the Rood, this is too much!" the merchant said, and, as Little John tossed the bag back at him after taking from it twenty gold marks, he took two quick steps forward, and dealt the giant a flat-handed blow at which he staggered and fell. A roar went up from the outlaws, and two men drew their swords as Little John got to his feet.

"Hold!" Robin Hood cried with a laugh. "He had the right of it. John, where were your manners, that you did not hand back the bag, for this is a man of substance, and no mere churl? Pick up the bag and give it to him as to a man worth respect."

"He hath a good muscle," Friar Tuck said, with a chuckle. "Merchant, will you try a game of buffets with me?"

"Willingly, if I knew the game," the merchant answered.

"A simple game," the friar assured him, coming forward. "See, now, you stand there, and I stand here. I give you such a buffet as you gave our infant John, who is too small and weak to stand such games, and if you can get on your feet again, you may give me one back." For Friar Tuck reckoned on avenging the mighty blow his friend had suffered.

"Strike, then," said the merchant, "I will play your game."

Friar Tuck rolled back his sleeve and gave the tall merchant such a blow as had sent many a man rolling, but it did not produce even a quiver of the merchant's frame.

"Saint Peter, but this is an iron merchant!" said the Friar. "Now smite, unless you be pegged to the ground."

The merchant gave him a careless wallop, and over he went like a ninepin. He got on his feet again in a dazed way.

"Enough, good merchant," he said, "for the Church is overthrown. But by the ringing in my head the bells are sound."

"My turn," Robin Hood said, a little nettled at seeing his two strongest men felled so easily. "Stand for it, merchant, while I give you a buffet, and then I will take one from you."

He put all his strength into his blow, and the merchant rocked on his feet a little and shook his head, as if the blow had been no light one. But, to Robin's surprise, he did not fall, though no one man of the band could keep on his feet after one of Robin's buffets.

"My turn," said the merchant, and Robin braced himself for the blow.

But, like Little John and the friar, he went spinning as the merchant's hat, shaken by the force he put into his blow, fell from his head. Robin got on his feet ruefully, and then saw who had struck the blow. He fell on one knee before the man who had struck him down.

"Sire," he said, "it is no disgrace to me to be laid low by the arm that wrought such wonders against the Saracens. And since the black knight and the palmer are now a merchant, we of Sherwood crave a royal pardon at the merchant's hands."

"Ha!" said Richard, "but what of the stolen deer? What of the prelates of the Church robbed, and the spoiling of my barons who passed this way? Why should I pardon you?"

Robin got on his feet. "Lord King," he said, "if I have spoiled such as Abbot Hugo, I have but taken the spoils of a thief. If I have robbed a baron, I have done no more harm. I have wronged no woman and harmed no man who lives justly."

"And will you be judge as to who lives justly?" King Richard asked.

"I will be judge of what I know," Robin answered hardily, looking his King in the face, "and deal justly when I have judged. I have spoiled a thieving Prior to send money to your ransom, that we might have a king worth serving in England. I have made oppressors afraid of their evil deeds, and lived cleanly in the greenwood while barons did foul things in castles. You, sire, know what manner of place was Evil Hold, that a certain black knight helped my men to assault."

"True—true enough," Richard answered moodily. "But what of the deer? There you have broken the laws."

"I confess our fault," Robin said frankly, "yet, outlawed as we were, how else could we live? Sire, these men have fought with you, and not one of them but has prayed for your return to this misruled land. Grant them pardon, and do as you will with me."

"Nay, Robin," the King answered with a smile, "all or none. Now this I will do for you. All that has been shall be forgotten, and you shall be restored every man to his rights, while I will make you warden of Sherwood, with such men as you may choose to serve under you, and with such pay as is fitting to the place. And if any men of your band choose to serve under me in France, then they may come with me, for I need good men to follow me there."

"Now, men," said Robin, "cheer your good King, for never has this England known such a king and fighter as our King Richard."

They responded with cheers that rang till the forest echoed, and Abbot Hugo, riding down toward Nottingham, forgot to curse over the loss of his gold while he spurred on at such a pace that his followers could hardly keep up with him. Friar Tuck led forward the supposed merchant's horse for him to mount.

"Lord King," he said, "I would that you had time to dine with us, now we are no longer outlaws, for then you might let fall some word that would teach me the secret of the blow that felled me."

"Let us give you escort to Nottingham," Robin urged.

But King Richard shook his head. "I travel alone and fast, on my way to France," he answered. "See that you brave men do loyally and touch the deer no more, for this night a free pardon for you all will lie in the hands of Robert de Rainault in Nottingham, and your inlawing shall be cried in every town in the county. So fare you well, Warden of Sherwood, and see that you do your duty till I come again."

And with a wave of his hand King Richard rode away, leaving them all standing bareheaded in the forest glen. Then with a sigh Little John turned to his leader.

"Where now, Robin?" he asked, "since our good days are done."

"Nay," said Robin, "for such as will may keep with me in our secret glade, and who keeps count of the game in Sherwood so well as the warden of the forest? So many head are my right each year, and we will have them, while since we are all rich men with the small things we have won, anyone who will may hire him land or take to the towns. But the greenwood for me."

A score of them elected to leave the band and settle down, but the rest kept to their leader, and went with him to receive from the Sheriff of Nottingham the parchment deed of their pardon. There was many a smile among them at Robert de Rainault's sour face as he handed the deed to Robin, for he had far rather have hanged his enemy.

"Sheriff," Robin said, "will you take back that arrow you signed?

The Sheriff shook his head. "Wait," he answered, "for kings do not live for ever."

CHAPTER 17 / How Guy of Gisborne Tried Again

THERE is an old ballad which tells that King Richard, when he pardoned Robin Hood and his band, took them to court with him to serve about him, but this cannot have been true. For Richard, landing in England after his ransom from the Austrian castle, spent but a few days in London before he went off to Lincolnshire and the Midlands to punish the worst of those who had followed John in his absence, and, when he returned to his capital, it was but to raise money and assemble his men for the journey to France from which he never returned. He spent only three months in England, at this time. So it is much more likely that he made Robin warden of Sherwood, knowing that he who had hunted the King's deer would know how to guard them from others.

He had not left England before Robert de Rainault, sore and angry over Robin's pardon, sought audience with Prince John and put before him what he called "this monstrous injustice" of the royal pardon for the outlaws. John nodded, understanding.

"Wait, Sheriff," he bade, "for our royal brother hath many matters on his hands at this time. You shall give me the names of these men, and I will send you a full deed of outlawry against them."

The Sheriff went back to Nottingham with a letter bearing John's signature, and bidding him proclaim Robin Hood and his men outlaws once more.

The news came like a thunderclap to the men of

the band. Much, the miller's son, whom Robin had put in charge of Locksley farm when he claimed it back as his right, was in Nottingham when the crier proclaimed the news, and all the city buzzed with excitement over it. Much went hastening back to Locksley, for he knew that Robin himself, with Marian, were due to visit him the next day, while there were the men about the farm to warn as well, lest they should be taken and hanged.

It was then late spring, and Much came back toward Locksley in the dusk of the evening, but with light enough to see the gleam of armour about the homestead. Guy of Gisborne, sent by the Abbot of St. Mary's, had laid an ambush about the place, but Much's forest training had made his eyes keen, and instead of making for Locksley he slid away into the forest, and made all the haste he could to the secret glen in which Robin and Marian still lived with their faithful followers round them.

"Good Robin," said Much, "we are all dead men."

"Say no more," said Robin, "for there is an old proverb that dead men tell no tales, yet here you come with a tale."

"Robin, the Sheriff of Nottingham hath proclaimed us all outlawed again, for I heard it cried in the city this day."

"He did that once before, but we were not dead for it then," Robin answered composedly.

"And St. Mary's hath set an ambush round Locksley homestead," Much went on with his tale, "to catch any of us who come there."

"Right good news," Robin answered. "I will twist Master Guy his tail for him, and, if these good men are willing, we will set an ambush round *his* home.

For if a good game is started, at least two should play at it, by all accounts."

"Robin, you seem no bit alarmed," Little John remarked.

"Alarmed?" Robin said, and laughed. "Nay, for while I have been warden of the forest, I have had but a certain number of the deer allotted to me for our eating. Now we have the lot, Little John, and other things as well that we have missed since we left off being outlaws."

"What will you do, then?" Little John asked.

"Well," said Robin, "first of all we will get Friar Tuck to roast the haunches of venison that we had hung up for to-morrow, for now we may take all we like. Next, we will roll out a fresh barrel of ale, for there is a wagon train of liquor due up from Newark next week, and it shall pay full toll to us. So we shall make ourselves a right merry feast, before we go to twist the tail of Guy of Gisborne."

Marian, seeing them talking, came out to them, and Robin put his arm round her affectionately.

"Dear girl," he said, "we are once more outlawed. Now will you that I send you to your father at Lea Castle, for safety?"

She laughed at him. "When you are tired of me, Robin, then you may send me away. Not before."

He kissed her tenderly. "Now tell Friar Tuck to cook his hardest, for we will all feast late this night," he bade. "Bid him take venison and spare not, for all is ours again. And at dawn we will set out for Gisborne grange."

"My part, methinks, lies in the tapping of that new barrel," Little John said. "Much, come and lend me a hand with it."

"Roll out two barrels, Much," Robin Hood added, "for if Little John and the friar get at one, there will be little left."

It was, as Robin had said, late when they began their feast, but there was an air of merriment and jollity about it which had been lacking of late. For, with King Richard overseas again, prelates and barons had felt themselves free to do as they liked with the common people, and as the King's man Robin had had to keep within the law, and let pass many an act of tyranny that he would have checked had he been outlawed and king of Sherwood, as he was now once again.

They had barely settled to their feast when in came Will Scarlett, who, since they had had the royal pardon, had gone into partnership with old Much the miller, but now, learning that he was not safe outside Sherwood, returned to Robin's band.

So they feasted, right merrily, with Marian to grace their feast, and Robin Hood revolving plans for the future.

In mid-morning of the next day Guy of Gisborne and his men tramped back, hungry and weary, from keeping useless watch on Locksley farm, for neither Much, whom they expected to find there, nor anyone else, had appeared for them to catch. Guy looked forward to rest and refreshment at his grange before going on to report to Abbot Hugo how the outlaws had got wind of his ambush too soon, but from behind a hedge nearly a quarter of a mile distant from his place some four score heads bobbed up as he came on with his men, and a flight of arrows sang about their ears and rattled on their harness. Except for three of them who went down, two with arrows through their legs and one shot in the shoulder, Guy's men turned and bolted for cover like shot rabbits, and Guy himself followed them.

"Stout fighter," Robin remarked. "In case he lose himself, we will light him a fire that he may see his way home."

And, taking half a dozen of his men while the rest kept watch for Guy and his followers, Robin marched to the grange, where the few serfs left fled at his approach, and set fire to the place. He left the ricks and cattle sheds untouched, but soon the stone house was wrapped in flames, which licked off the thatch and poured skywards in a dense column of black smoke.

And thus ended Guy's second attempt at catching Robin Hood, which, since the grange was the property of St. Mary's Abbey, left Abbot Hugo a very angry man, swearing vengeance.

CHAPTER 18 / The Named Arrow

Now, although Robin Hood and his men were again proclaimed outlaws, they had so many friends that it was not considered safe to touch them in any way, for all knew that King Richard had given them a free pardon, and only the ill-will of the Sheriff Robert and Abbot Hugo were to blame for this second proclamation. Some day, people said, King Richard would come back.

So the time went by, until the grievous news came from overseas that King Richard had been struck down by an arrow before the castle of Chaluz, and had died of the wound, at which Robin and his men mourned for the loss of a good king.

One summer morn, when King Richard had been dead over two years, one of Robin's men came to him hastily where he hunted in the forest not far from Nottingham itself. And, at the news his man brought, Robin sounded a call on his horn, and in a matter of minutes had two score of his followers round him, all armed with their bows and swords.

"Here is no time to lose," he told them, "for Robert de Rainault hath captured our Little John and takes him in to Nottingham to hang him."

"Where is the Sheriff?" Will Scarlett asked.

"Now on his way to Nottingham with his prisoner," Robin answered. "There are enough of us to rescue our man, for if once he get into Nottingham jail, it will be a hard task to save him from the hangman. Let us away to the track."

As he went, he took the arrows out from his quiver and looked them over, selecting one that he had kept for years now. On it the Sheriff had written his name, when Robin let him go and he failed to keep his promise regarding the sum for his ransom.

Little John, it seemed, had been alone when they took him, and the man who came to Robin Hood with the news of his capture had seen the Sheriff, with a party of armed men, riding down toward Nottingham with his prisoner tied to his own saddle, with hands bound behind him.

They came to the track, and saw by the hoofmarks on it that the Sheriff and his men had not yet gone back to Nottingham. Then Robin placed his men, and waited a full half hour, for he was determined to save his brave man from the Sheriff's grasp.

Noon had passed before the clinking of harness and a murmur of voices warned Robin's men that the Sheriff was on his way toward them, and then they saw him, with Little John bound and dragged along by a rope that bound him to the Sheriff's horse, and nearly fifty men-at-arms following their master. Robin saw that Little John could scarcely walk, and without challenge or any word he crashed an arrow into the horse's head, so that it fell dead on the track, and the Sheriff barely got clear of it as it dropped, but drew his sword.

"Ha! Ambush!" he cried. "At them, my men."

His men were Normans, sturdy and dogged, and Robin knew that they outnumbered his own party. But Robin's second arrow dropped one of them, and six others went down under the outlaws' shooting before they drew their swords and charged in, fiercely determined on rescuing their giant comrade. It was a fight fierce and fell.

Every man of Robin's party fought like a hero. Now a dozen of the Sheriff's men were down, and ten of Robin's band, and Will Scarlett, striking at one, was himself struck from behind by the Sheriff, who laid him low over the body of his own man. At that Robin found time to draw back from the fighting and get out the arrow he had kept, for this foul stroke at his man enraged him, and he had loved Will Scarlett almost as much as Little John himself.

"Remember the signed arrow, Sheriff!" he cried as he loosed the string.

The arrow sped to its mark, and crashed full in Robert de Rainault's forehead. By that time half of Robin's men were down, and more than half of the Sheriff's party, though they were more heavily armed and ready for the fight, since the outlaws had come to it in hunting trim, with no thought of a battle.

But, at the Sheriff's fall, panic seized on his men, who fled as best they could—such of them as were able to flee. Arrows followed them in their flight, and on that day Robin himself, raging at the loss of Will Scarlett, who moved no more after the Sheriff's foul stroke, accomplished one of his most noted feats of archery. For there was one of the Sheriff's men who had won almost to the gate of Nottingham itself when, from nearly a mile away, a long shaft from Robin's bow laid him lifeless, last to fall of the party who had dared to measure swords against Robin Hood and his men in fair fight.

They loosed Little John's bonds, and found him so sorely hurt that they had to carry him to their stronghold, where he was weeks recovering from his wound. Will Scarlett they buried in the greenwood, and Robin mourned over the loss of a gallant fighter and true friend. Eighteen of Robin's men, it is said, died that day, while of the Sheriff's party near on thirty never came back to tell the tale.

But those who did win back to Nottingham told that they had nearly exterminated the outlaws, and that Robin himself had been sorely wounded. For they had to cover up their defeat by giving the number of their assailants as far greater than it was, and so the word went round that the outlaws of Sherwood were broken men, their leader sorely wounded, and their numbers so reduced that the forest might easily be cleared of them.

Among those who heard this story was Abbot Hugo, brother of the dead Sheriff, who, when he had said masses for the repose of Robert de Rainault's soul, after attending his funeral at Nottingham, called to him Guy of Gisborne for a conference.

"Time after time I have sent you against this outlaw, Guy," he said, "and each time he hath shamed you. But now, I think, we have him."

"You would have me go after him again, Lord Abbot?" Guy asked.

The Abbot nodded. "We will have vengeance for my brother's death," he said, "the more so since the arrow that slew him, being marked with his name, points clearly to murder."

"How will you that I take him?" Guy asked. "For if I go hunting in Sherwood for him, I may hunt a year, and never find a sign of him. He knows the forest too well."

"Nay," said Hugo, "that is work wasted. But do

you get together our men-at-arms, of whom we can muster over forty, and say nothing of our intent. I will cause it to be given out that, at the end of next week, I am sending the tax money for our King John down to Nottingham, for that money must be sent. It shall go under guard of five armed men only."

"Ah!" said Guy. "That will be the bait."

The Abbot nodded. "That will be the bait," he agreed, "and you shall be the trap. For we know by all reports that there are not a score of these outlaws left now, and you shall follow on the party with the gold by half an hour. When Robin Hood and his men are busy over the spoil, you and your men can fall on them, and strike and spare not."

Guy nodded agreement.

CHAPTER 19 / The Tale of Alan-a-Dale

ROBIN HOOD was out hunting in the forest one morning early, and, crossing the tract that led down to Meden Dale, he spied a youth sitting on a fallen tree, with a harp lying beside him. The youth wore clothing that had once been rich and fine, but now was muddy and uncared for, and as he sat he warbled a mournful ditty, heedless of the tall figure of Robin, who watched and listened.

"A good voice," said Robin, when the warbling ceased, "but a poor use for it. Why sit there and yowl like a cat on a branch? Who are you?"

"Alan from Meden Dale—they call me Alan-a-Dale," said the youth. "This should have been my wedding-day, but to-day the fair Eleanor, my lady-love, must marry Sir Ralph of Warsop, a rich old scoundrel of a baron against her will, when she longed to marry me. At the little Norman church in Meden Dale they will marry her to him in four hours' time, and there is naught left for me to do but sit and sing a dirge."

"Nay, there is much else to be done, good Alan," Robin responded, and unslung his silver bugle, with which he blew a call.

"A pretty note," said Alan, "but what will it do?"

Before Robin could answer, Little John broke out from the undergrowth, an arrow on the string. Then came Friar Tuck, brandishing his quarter-staff, and after them man after man, until over forty were assembled round Robin and Alan-a-Dale, wondering what the alarm was about.

"Friends," Robin said, "we will go a-marrying, down in Meden Dale. Sir Ralph of Warsop is marrying a fair damsel called Eleanor—at least, he thinks he is marrying her, till we get there. But you must prink up a bit for this wedding, good Alan, for we would not have you go to it looking like a blue jay after a fight with a cat."

"I have no wish to go to the wedding," Alan said.

"Nay, but you will when we have told you what I plan to do," Robin said with a smile. "Here and let me tell you."

So Alan listened, and the smile on the face of Little John grew broader as he heard, while Friar Tuck chuckled aloud.

But three hours later the bells of the little Norman church in Meden Dale began to peal joyfully, and old Sir Ralph, pompous in silks and gold-laced velvets, entered the church at the head of a dozen or more gorgeously attired retainers, to wait by the altar for his bride. When Sir Ralph had waited nearly half an hour, the bride's father led her into the church, a pale, unwilling girl who could see no way of escape from her doom.

The church was more than half filled with watchers, and against a pillar not far from the altar leaned a tall man wrapped in a cloak, which seemed strange on this summer day. As Eleanor's father led her to the altar the tall man looked at her curiously, and saw that her eyes were red from much weeping.

Then, just as she reached Sir Ralph's side, the tall man flung back his cloak and lifted a silver bugle to his lips, with which he blew a shrill blast that drowned the voice of the priest, who had already begun the words of the marriage ceremony. And, at the sound, three-quarters of the men in the church rose up and surged toward the altar, while both the bride's father and old Sir Ralph gasped in amazement. But the tall man with the bugle, who was none other than Robin Hood, grasped Sir Ralph by his shoulder and dragged him away, thrusting him back to Little John, who gripped him by the ear and held him.

"What means this outrage—this sacrilege?" the bride's father demanded.

"Nay," said Robin, "for we do but prevent the sacrilege of bargaining away a fair maid to an old villain who hath already buried three wives, and will soon, we hope, be buried himself. Hold him tight, Little John, and twist his ear if he wriggles. Now Alan-a-Dale, are you willing to wed the fair Eleanor?"

"Right joyfully," said Alan, who had come to stand where Sir Ralph had stood beside her.

"And you, Eleanor," Robin pursued, "is it your will to marry Alan-a-Dale, in place of this bald-headed peacock?"

She murmured her assent, and took Alan's hand.

"Then proceed with the work, priest," Robin bade, "and see that you make a good job of it. We will have Sir Ralph here to witness the ceremony. Nay, Sir Ralph, keep quiet, or I will cuff your one ear while Little John holds the other! Proceed with the business, priest."

"That I cannot," the priest said quaveringly, "for the banns have not been called between these two."

"Easily remedied," Robin said. "Friar Tuck? Where are you, you fat old ale barrel? Call me the banns between Alan-a-Dale and the fair Eleanor!"

At that Friar Tuck waddled forth and climbed up into the singing loft, where he cried the banns three times, and came down again.

"Now all is in order," Robin said to the priest. "Proceed with the ceremony, priest, for we have witnesses here a-plenty."

"Who giveth this maid?" the priest asked shakily.

"I, Robin Hood, give her to this man," Robin answered, taking no notice of her father, "and any man who should dare to stand between her and Alan-a-Dale must reckon with me."

Then the priest married them, and after the ceremony Robin claimed the first kiss from the bride, who gave it willingly, having thus unexpectedly won happiness instead of misery with old Sir Ralph. After that, Robin and his men escorted the bride and bridegroom to Alan's home, a stout stone house in the midst of spacious, fertile lands, and Alan's mother kissed his bride and welcomed her gladly, for already the news of the wedding had reached her.

Then Alan's serving men and women made a feast for the outlaws, and Friar Tuck sang them what he called a song while Alan played his harp. Right merrily they feasted while the summer sun went down, after which Robin Hood gathered his men together, and they said good-bye to the bride and bridegroom, since the outlaws had miles to go to their hold.

"But remember," Alan bade them, "there is always an open door and a welcome for any man of you who comes this way."

"As there is in the forest for you and your fair bride," Robin answered. "We will look to see you visiting us, before many days have passed."

"But how shall I find you?" Alan asked.

"Sit on a log and yowl," Robin bade, "and we will know who it is without more telling. Yowl but loudly, and you will not lack a guide to our retreat, where my wife Marian will give your bride a hearty welcome."

Not many weeks had passed before Alan sat on a log and carolled forth a song, and, after that, he and Eleanor were often the guests of the outlaws, who, in their turn, came to look on Alan as in some way one of themselves, and often found their way to his hospitable home.

THE sun shone brightly on Sherwood's glades when
Abbot Hugo sent his convoy, as he had planned,
toward Nottingham, confident that Robin Hood and
his men would come out after it, and thus render
themselves easy prey for Guy of Gisborne and the
party who followed on after the pack mules. And, up
to a point, the plan worked well enough, for when
the friars with the mules were still two miles away
from Nottingham gate, a body of outlaws broke out
of the forest shades and surrounded them.

"Now stand, you shavelings," said Friar Tuck, who
led the attacking party, "for that cargo needs over-
hauling."

"Shaveling yourself," retorted Anselm, Abbot
Hugo's clerk, in charge of the party. "Here be holy
relics that we bear to St. Ninian's church in Nottingham, against the festival of harvest. Dare not to
commit sacrilege by laying hands on them!"

"Relics?" the jolly Friar replied. "We will leave
you your relics and all gear of that sort, so fear not
for them."

They laid out the stores that the mules carried,
and found good flour ground in Abbot Hugo's mills,
a couple of bags of gold marks, store of cloth and
fine linen, and sundry other rich goods that Abbot
Hugo had sent, never doubting that Guy and his
men would see them safely through, as presents for
the new Sheriff of Nottingham, Simon Ganmere, who

had been appointed in consequence of Robert de Rainault's death at the hands of Robin Hood. There was also a letter that Anselm the clerk carried, which Much, having searched the clerk, handed to Friar Tuck to read.

The friar read it aloud for the outlaws to hear.

"To Simon Ganmere, greeting and good will, from our Abbey of St. Mary's. I send with this sundry presents, and bespeak your presence at my Abbey to a banquet that I will hold on any day that may please you. If things fall out as I have planned them, this day will the villian outlaw, Robin Hood, be captured or killed by my steward, Guy of Gisborne, and if he should be captured alive it is my will that Guy bring him to you at Nottingham, that you may hang him over the city gate, as warning to all rogues of his kind. Also I think that Guy my man will dispose of most of the outlaws who yet remain.

"But, since some may escape to be a terror to honest men, I trust that you, Sheriff, will root them out of the forest and burn their hold, so that the ways may be free again when we have cause to travel by Sherwood on our errands. And most heartily do I trust that Guy of Gisborne may take this Robin Hood alive, for it would please me most mightily if he were hanged like a common felon, rather than killed in fight.

"Now again I send you right hearty greeting, and the hope that you may accept these poor presents of mine with my good will. Given at our Abbey of St. Mary's by Hugo, Abbot."

"A right cheerful epistle," said Friar Tuck, when he

had finished reading, "and I doubt not that it will please our Robin to hear it read again. Put all the goods back on the mules, lads, and trouble not whether there is a stray finger nail or a shoe lace or two over, after this. And we, being bursting with good will, like Abbot Hugo, will truss these shaven rascals like chickens, with gags to stop their squealing, and place them gently away from the track, lest they should be found too easily, while we go and see what good Robin and the rest of the band are doing."

Six men went off with the mules to the outlaws' secret hold, while Anselm and the other monks, submitting to being bound and gagged because they could not help it, still hoped to see Guy of Gisborne ride down on the outlaws and put them to flight, before all was done. But they waited in vain, for there was no sound nor sign of Guy or any man.

A mile behind them, Guy of Gisborne had led on twenty mounted men, and thirty men on foot, till they came to a point where not more than three of them could ride abreast, and the undergrowth on either side was too dense for a man to force his way through. Suddenly, as they rode, a great tree trunk crashed down across the track before them, barring the way, since it was too big for a horse to leap, and as the horses shied back in alarm a second trunk fell with a thud behind, so that they were in a sort of pen, horse and foot together.

Ahead of them, beyond the foremost fallen trunk, Robin Hood stepped out into view, and a dozen crossbows were instantly levelled at him. But not a bolt was shot, for a flight of great arrows whizzed before the crossbowmen could take aim, and Abbot Hugo was short of a dozen men that moment.

"And so for the next man who would shoot," said Robin calmly, as he advanced close to the great log across the way. " 'Tis a great while since we two have had a word with each other, Guy, and I have a mind to talk with you alone, with a sword or two between us to point our speech."

Now Guy, who had counted on outnumbering Robin's men by two to one, saw outlaws swarm out from the forest depths to watch over their leader, and knew himself and his men outnumbered, while already he had seen how deadly were the arrows of his opponents.

"I yield me," he said sullenly. "You have outwitted me again, and I would not waste the lives of good men any more."

"Have no fear," Robin assured him, "for my men can take care of themselves. No good men will suffer, though those Norman hogs behind you may be sorry for themselves."

"Robin!" called Friar Tuck from behind him, waddling up with the letter he had taken from Anselm in his hand. "Hold them yet a minute while I read you this. 'Tis from Abbot Hugo to the new Sheriff at Nottingham."

He read the letter aloud, translating it to Norman-French as he read, so that Guy of Gisborne's men might hear and understand it. Robin and most of his men understood that tongue as well as English, and Robin's face darkened as he heard what Hugo had written.

"There is a new face on this business," he said, "for

this talk of hanging is not to my taste. Guy of Gisborne, you heard?"

"Aye, I have heard," Guy answered, "and stand by it."

"For my part, I have a mind to end this matter here," Robin said with deadly calm, for the letter had angered him past bearing. "Now do you get down and climb over that log with your sword, leaving your men where they are, for I have no quarrel with them, poor fools. Here you and I will fight it out, with these men of mine to see fair play, and so shall we end this long quarrel once and for all."

"And if I win the fight, what happens to me?" Guy asked.

"You go back to Abbot Hugo, and tell him how you have made an end of me," Robin Hood answered.

"And if I will not fight you so?" Guy asked again.

"Then in the hearing of your men I name you coward, unworthy to be followed by the meanest knave that breathes," Robin said fiercely. "Twice you have come against me, and twice have I let you go back alive to your master. Now, this third time, we settle it for all time. Get down from your horse."

After one more moment's hesitation Guy dismounted, handed his horse over to his men, and clambered over the log, after which he drew his sword. Robin, with his men in a ring about him, faced his old enemy.

"To the death, Guy," he said.

"To the death," Guy of Gisborne echoed.

Then they set to, fighting warily at first, so that the great blades slithered along each other with a grinding noise as they guarded each other's blows and thrusts. And it chanced that Robin trod on a thick twig as he stepped back, so that it rolled under his foot, and he slipped a little. The point of Guy's sword just nicked his neck above his doublet, drawing blood.

"Aha!" said Guy. "Nearly!"

"Nearly, fool, is not quite," Robin responded. "Guard!"

And Guy was in time, but only just in time, to save himself from Robin's recovery and resulting thrust.

Now they had fought a good ten minutes, and both were breathing hard, for the work grew hot and fierce. Presently Robin leaped in air as Guy tried the old Norse trick of sweeping at his knees, and by that the steward of St. Mary's sealed his own doom. For, ere he could get his blade aloft, Robin struck, and with one great backhanded blow laid Guy of Gisborne dead.

He stood back. "An end," he said. "Peace to him, though he served a bad master, and himself had no pity on those he ruled."

"And next, mighty Robin Hood?" Friar Tuck asked.

"Haul up the logs to let these men and horses go," Robin answered, "but first strip them to their shirts, as once before we did with the men whom Guy of Gisborne led against us. Then let them take him and these other dead back to St. Mary's Abbey, and pin that letter of the Abbot's on the breast of dead Guy, that he may know how his message hath fared."

Now came peace in Sherwood, for King John and the barons were too busy fighting each other to spare men for clearing off Robin Hood's band, and Simon Ganmere, the new Sheriff of Nottingham, though he sent bodies of men after them once or twice, got worsted so much that, rather than make himself a laughing-stock, he left them alone.

So the years passed, and the merry men hunted the deer and took toll of prelates and barons as they would.

But in St. Mary's Abbey, Hugo de Rainault remembered the death of his brother at Robin Hood's hands; he remembered, too, how Robin had set free Sir Richard at Lea, and so had shamed him before King Richard. Altogether, Abbot Hugo had a long count against the great outlaw, and he nursed his hate and waited, meanwhile growing old.

He could see no way of getting even with his enemy, for never could any man find the way to Robin's secret glade in the depths of Sherwood; those who knew it would not betray the men who were their friends, and, lacking that knowledge, Hugo knew it as useless to send men into the forest depths. While he brooded and grew old the world went its accustomed way. Still the outlaw band throve in Sherwood, and hunted the deer in its glades.

Abbot Hugo was quite an old man when he was

told, one day, that a chapman or pedlar desired to see him, and bade that the man should be admitted to his presence. In came a thin little man, and, when he had put down the pack and looked at Hugo with narrow, crafty eyes, the Abbot stared hard at him.

"That," he said, "should be the face of Roger le Gran, if the years had not changed it so."

"It is, Abbot," Roger called "the Cruel" answered. "Once a knight, but, since Robin Hood and his men burnt out Castle Belame, a beggared man living how I can."

"Well," the Abbot said, "I cannot help you, Roger, for that same Robin hath stripped me of so much of my wealth that I am but a poor man, now."

"But how if I could help you?" Roger asked. "You cannot hate this Robin more than I hate him. What if I find you a way to his hold, and guide your men there to destroy it?"

"Can you do this?" Hugo asked eagerly.

Roger nodded. "I think I see a way," he answered. "What will you give me if I do it?"

"If I knew that all the band of them were destroyed," Hugo answered slowly, "I would give half the spoil that they have amassed, and five hundred gold marks as well—enough to make you the richest man between here and Nottingham, friend Roger."

Roger nodded. "I do not know the way to their hold yet," he said, "but I think there is a way by which I may find it. It needs but that I travel there and return once, for I never forget a road I have trodden."

"But how will you get there?" Hugo asked.

"Hark ye, Abbot," Roger responded, "and I will tell my plan."

Next day the outlaws had fed full well in their glade, as was their custom, and Friar Tuck, fatter and more jovial than ever, had declared that if he had only drunk two quarts less of ale with his venison, Little John would never have beaten him at the good game of quarter-staff. Down into the glade, toward evening, came Will the Pedlar, an old friend of the band, who often brought his pack to see if they would buy of him, and generally brought them news as well. With him came a stranger, also with a pack on his back, at sight of whom Little John stepped forward.

"How now, Will?" Little John asked. "You know well that no strangers may learn the way to our retreat."

"But this is an honest rascal, your worship," Will answered, "and he hath a goodly store of right curious trinkets, Arabian daggers, a hunting knife that the Soldan of Syria used, and like marvels. I vouch for him being a right good man, and safe to bring to your hold."

"Let be, then, since he is here," Little John growled, "but you are surety for his honesty, remember."

One thing that Will the Pedlar did not tell Little John was that the stranger had given him five good gold marks for permission to accompany him to the glade. The new-comer spread out his wares, and soon had the outlaws chaffering with him, while the wives of such as lived married in the glade came to buy ornaments, which the chapman offered at such ridiculously cheap rates that presently the news came to Marian, Robin's wife.

"I think I will go and see this chapman," she said, "in case he have any trinkets left that I should like."

The evening was growing old, then, and, as she went out from the home that she had shared with Robin for years now, she saw the strange chapman rolling up his pack, as if to depart. But she went up to him, in case any of his goods should be left unsold.

"Good chapman," she asked courteously, "may I not see your wares?"

He looked up at her, and on the instant she knew the face of Roger the Cruel, which she had last seen when Isambart held her prisoner in Evil Hold. No other among the outlaw band knew his face, for always they had seen him in armour, and with visor down, but Marian knew him, and at sight of his evil eyes she turned to cry out a warning. But Roger leaped at her, drawing his dagger, and struck her down, so that her cry was a scream of pain.

At the sound men came to the doors of their huts in the glade, and Robin, knowing that it was Marian who had cried, snatched at his bow and ran out to aid her. He saw her lying helpless, and saw the figure of a man running madly toward the cliff path in the dusk, and at that he put an arrow on the string. The distance was great and the light uncertain, but the arrow was sped by the best archer who ever drew string beside his ear in all England.

The speeding arrow took Roger in the shoulder as he brushed by a sapling, and pinned him to the tree in such fashion that he could not move for the pain that movement gave him. By this time a dozen men were running toward Marian, but Robin, easily out-

distancing them, pointed to the figure on the cliff path.

"Let be," he said, "and fetch that man back. I will see to my own wife while you get him."

And he ran to Marian, lifting her in his arms. Her wound, he could tell, was too deep for any aid to save her, and she herself knew that she was dying. She smiled up at him.

"This, methinks, is our farewell, lover of mine," she said weakly, "for in a little time I shall be gone. But before I go, I would thank you for all the happy years."

Robin bent his head and kissed her. "Dear wife," he said brokenly, "I had looked for many more happy years, but now is life robbed of its chief joy, and I go sorrowing all my days."

"There is left you green Sherwood, Robin mine," she told him, "and I shall watch over you. Now call our Friar that I may have the last rites of the church, and do you hold me."

So Robin held her while Friar Tuck, with tears running down his cheeks, administered to her, and then left them. What they said to each other in the last minutes no man knew, except for one sentence of hers that Robin told Little John and Friar Tuck after.

"So, she said, she would have had it," he said, "to die in the heart of the greenwood with my arms round her, and the evening light fading. And never had man truer or more loyal wife than this my Marian, whom I shall mourn until I go to join her."

Now, before the light had altogether gone, they brought back Roger the Cruel, but by that time Robin had borne the body of Marian away, and returned to stand with folded arms, grimly waiting to face the murderer. While he waited, Will the Pedlar flung himself at the outlaw's feet.

"Mercy, Robin!" he whined, "for I thought him a true man, else I had not let him come with me."

"This mercy," Robin answered calmly. "Get you gone, nor ever let me see your face again, or I may remember how my wife died through you."

Will slunk away, and fled out of Nottinghamshire altogether soon after, for the story went about how he had brought to the outlaws' hold the man who murdered the queen of Sherwood.

But Robin and his men took Roger the Cruel and marched through the night with him, for they had found on him a paper by which the Abbot of St. Mary's promised him half the spoil of the secret glade, and five hundred marks as well, in return for guidance to their hiding place. Roger had not trusted the Abbot's word, but had claimed the paper before he would go to search out the way.

As they went, Robin's men hewed down great poles from the forest trees, which they took with them, and, fifty yards from the gate of St. Mary's Abbey, they set up a gallows of these poles, and on it hanged Roger the Cruel, with the Abbot's parchment of promise sewn on his breast, that all men might see. Across the foot of it Friar Tuck had written at Robin's bidding:

"This doom to Abbot Hugo's hireling murderer. When next Abbot Hugo goes abroad, the doom will find him too."

After which threat, Abbot Hugo never left the Abbey grounds, for he knew that Robin Hood kept his word always.

But, after Marian's death, things were never the same in the glade, for all had loved her, and all mourned her loss, while Robin Hood himself was inconsolable. He divided up the wealth they had won among the men of his band, and bade them reckon themselves free to go where they would.

Some went to take service with Alan-a-Dale, who was still their good friend, and some went to Sir Richard at Lea, now grown old, but still giving every man of Robin's a welcome. Some went to the wars and fought in the battles that lasted till Simon de Montfort fell at Evesham, and some hired land and settled down to tell of the good days that had been in Sherwood.

When all was done, and Friar Tuck had gone to hermitage near by a noble trout stream and within bowshot of certain deer of Sherwood, Robin took down his bow and quiver and buckled his sword about his waist, while Little John watched and wondered.

"How now, good Robin?" Little John asked.

"Wherever the winds may blow me, or chance call me, there I shall go," Robin answered. "Do you make shift as have the rest, for our good days in Sherwood are done now that we grow old."

"Where you go, I go," said Little John, "for we have been friends too long to part by any wish of mine, until death parts us."

"We will go North, then," Robin said, "and I will count I have not lived in vain if you set such store by my friendship, good John."

"Think of the times we have known together," Little John said wistfully. "The good days when we sent Guy's band home in their shirts, and tricked the Sheriff and all the rest, and burned Evil Hold——

"And how great King Richard talked with you and gave you pardon, and how we spoiled the Abbot—aye, Robin, we have known too much together ever to part company."

So they went North, toward the Yorkshire border, but the spirit was out of bold Robin Hood since his dear wife's death, and a sickness fell on him as they travelled, so that when they came to Kirklees Abbey he besought the Abbess Elizabeth to give him shelter and a bed till he should be well enough to go on his way, at which she gave him a bed in a cell and tended him, while Little John stayed with him and slept before the door, lest there should be any treachery. Twice the Abbess bled Robin for his sickness, but it seemed to do him little good, and while he lay there Abbot Hugo of St. Mary's got word that he was in the power of the Abbess. At that Hugo wrote to the woman, who, though he did not know it, was sister to Robin's mother, else Robin had not reckoned himself safe there, since Kirklees was under the government of Abbot Hugo of St. Mary's.

A day after she had received Hugo's letter, the Abbess came to Robin's bedside and looked down at him thoughtfully.

"Nephew Robin, I must bleed you again, if you would get well."

"Be it as you will," he answered weakly.

She took a lancet and opened a vein, though in her heart she knew well that he was too weak for any more bleeding. Yet Abbot Hugo had laid a command on her, and though Robin was her own sister's son she obeyed.

Something in her eyes told him her intent, and he called out weakly, at which Little John, who had been waiting outside the window for the Abbess to go, entered the room. Robin signed to him.

"Put her out, and bind up my arm," he bade, "though I fear it is too late."

The Abbess left them, and Little John bound up the vein quickly. But he saw that Robin's lips were almost white, and heard how his breath came with fluttering swiftness. It was the end, Little John knew, and tears came in his eyes as he looked at his great master thus smitten down by a treacherous woman's hand.

All that afternoon Little John watched by the bed. Sometimes Robin talked to him of old times, and again his mind wandered, so that he thought himself in Sherwood with Marian, and with his good men round him. Toward evening he dozed awhile, and, wakening, looked up at Little John and smiled.

"John," he said, "I am going to see my sweet Marian, for she came to me in a dream and told me —told me—but I cannot tell you all she told me, old friend. Only, bring me my bow, and an arrow from the quiver."

Wondering, Little John brought the bow, and Robin laid the arrow to the string. The window casement was open, and Robin, sitting up in his bed, drew back the cord and shot the arrow through into the greenwood beyond the Abbey wall.

"There," he said, as he fell back in the bed, "there bury me, Little John, where the good green trees will rustle over me, and the birds sing when the year is young and fresh. Now bid me good-bye, for I would go. Marian, my Marian!"

With her name for his last word he died, and Little John wept beside the bed. But, before it was wholly dark, Little John went out and found the arrow, fallen under a great oak beyond the Abbey walls, and there he buried his master.

And Little John went out across the wolds, wandering always and telling tales of his friend and master, until he too died, though like Robin Hood he lives to this day in the hearts of those who love tales of loyalty and great deeds. To such as these, Robin Hood and his merry men will never die, though the dust of many years is blown above their graves.